Improve Your English Using English Idioms.

A full thirty lesson (600 idiom) course with examples, questions & answers.

PLUS: An easy to follow methodology

written by

Prof. Stephen W. Bradeley Bsc. (Hons)

Improve Your English Using English Idioms.

A full thirty lesson (600 idiom) course with examples, questions & answers.

PLUS: An easy to follow methodology

written by

Prof. Stephen W. Bradeley Bsc. (Hons)

Table of Contents

Preface

I'm Pleased You Want To Improve Your English?

Six Hundred Common English Idioms & Vocabulary in English with Portuguese translations.

This system of language teaching was designed to be used as a simple way for teachers or travellers to earn some extra money by teaching English. Some years ago whilst travelling. found the need to be able to make some extra money to help me pay for my living expenses whilst away from home. It gave me the freedom to travel at the same time I was able to carry the tools I needed to be able to offer the locals English classes.

You could store the files on your computer, keep them on a memory stick or keep them stored on a cloud storage system and then download and print as needed.

You may not print or copy the files to give to other teachers. I have offered the system at a very affordable price and so unauthorized copying is unnecessary.

There are nearly one million words in the English language according to the most recent (2014) Oxford English Dictionary. This course aims to give the student a comprehensive hold on the English language we use every day.

This book contains lessons one to thirty of the thirty lesson. There are six hundred idioms listed in this e-book.

Dedicated to my wife Rose who set me on this path.

An original Method of Teaching English

Listen - Repeat - Learn - Speak

Introduction

Welcome and congratulations on choosing this method of teaching and learning English. As a brief introduction to this methodology it will be useful first to talk about why we decided to write a new method, when there are so many very good methods already on the market.

First of all, having had personal experience of many methods in use throughout my teaching career and inheriting students from other schools suffering from frustration because of the lack of real achievement in the ability to communicate effectively in the new language. In a nutshell, we found that students coming to us through recommendation were all saying the same thing, that is, that after a significant number of months or even years studying they were still lacking in communicative ability.

Of course I'm being polite and what I really mean by this is that students have spent a lot of money without achieving any useful end product.
Learning any new language can be time consuming, frustrating and at best expensive.
So when choosing a school or self-help system, the priority must be effectiveness, because an effective methodology will ensure that both time and financial efficiency will not be a worry.
To this end, we have kept both of these principle considerations at the forefront whilst putting this book together. Students undertaking this method of study will learn English as quickly as is, humanly possible.

Thus, the method features three main areas.

1). ***Economy of time***. A student will be required to devote at least two hours per week of in-class study with a desired frequency of three hours per week. Of course there will also be a certain amount of home study which is most important. We have tried to keep this to a minimum. Each class will last for around forty minutes. During those forty minutes the student will be required to read the previous lesson back to the teacher. This will show the teacher that home study has taken place. This will normally last five minutes. Secondly, the new lesson will be introduced. Again this will take approximately a further fifteen minutes. Then thirdly, the student will be required to write a short text dictated by the teacher. This will take a further 10 minutes. Lastly, the student will have a ten minute two-way discussion period, where the student can air any concerns about this or the previous lesson content. Plus, this gives a few minutes' in-between classes or students. Total tuition time is approximately forty-five minutes.

2). ***Economy of cost***. Simply put, if the methodology is followed methodically then the student will achieve quickly and save money and time by cutting down on the time needed to learn the new language.

3). ***Making it easy***. The first thing we believe will overwhelm a student and cause him or her to **"drop out"** will be too much work, Ill explained concepts and or over complicated grammar will result in eventual boredom and the possibility of drop-out. We have tried to address all of these

attrition outcomes. Work and concepts will be offered to the student in "bite-size" chunks. Each forty minute lesson will have what we believe is relevant and consumable amounts of information that will allow the student to progress in the relevant direction at a satisfying and rewarding pace. Leading to conversation and understanding as quickly as possible.

In terms of total time commitment, we believe that a total of two hundred and twenty hours from none-speaker to effective but basic conversation and good understanding is reasonable, which of course includes time for end of stage tests which last one hour at the end of each nine lesson period and periodic twenty minute feedback assessments. This means that if a student attends school to study twice or home-study twice each week, then approximately two years will be the effective study period.

Each lesson, apart from having the content of the last lesson reviewed, a new lesson introduction, a dictation and discussion, should consist of a limited and precise number of new words and concepts in a logical and well thought out manner.

A key aspect to this method is ***"keeping it light"*** We believe that making the lessons fun with total interaction in both directions is of the utmost importance. We believe that if you can laugh together we can learn together. A moment of fun will reinforce the memory and help in the long term learning effect. So, we encourage student–teacher-student interaction within the classroom. The skill of the teacher is encouraged in a way that, if required. He or she can at will, when needed and relevant, change direction using personal experiences and fun examples to reinforce a particular point or concept.

At this point it is important to state that our overall aim is to be as effective and real-life as possible, whilst ensuring that the student finishes the course with all the grammatical tools needed to communicate effectively. Whether that be at work, socializing or on holiday.

Course Structure

Below is an explanation of how the book and course is structured. A total of thirty lessons.

Extra Classes to compliment this course.

Using this method you will also be able to offer extras in the mid to later stages of your course. The extras include the following:

Basic English For Business

This course is aimed at students who are already able to have a higher than basic conversation in English. It teaches simple terminology used in the workplace. These lessons are available to purchase as an extra.

English Fixed Expressions

A fixed expression in English is a standard form of expression that has taken on a more specific meaning than the expression itself. Fixed expressions are very common in English. These lessons are added as an extra and are available to purchase

English Idioms

An English idiom is a group of words established by usage as having a meaning not deducible from those of the individual words. For example “A bird’s eye view”

Exam and test structure (Main Course only) see the book list at end of this book.

We also have very well structured mid-stage tests and end of stage test structures. You will note that each stage is structured into nine lessons and each lesson if effectively covered twice.

Therefore, at the end of each three lessons covered (six sessions), there will be a short twenty minutes informal test which consists of ten simple yes or no questions to review the last six lessons. Which measures the student’s ability to memorise, listen and recognise the new words and concepts covered over the last six formal lessons (effectively three lessons covered twice). Plus, a very short dictation which includes some of the new words and concepts covered. The short dictation measures the student’s ability to recognise words verbally and then copy those words onto paper using the correct spelling and grammar. These two sections help to assess the students listening and understanding.

At the end of each full stage, consisting of nine lessons covered twice (effectively eighteen hours of work) the student will undergo a one-hour informal test consisting of thirty YES or NO questions to measure listening.

Thirty translations in the form of offering the student thirty of the new words in English and the student writing the translation in his or her own language. Then finally, a short dictation of around one hundred and fifty words covering concepts, meanings and words introduced during the previous weeks or months study.

Three short tests
The end of the first six lessons (20 minutes)
The end of the first twelve lessons (20 minutes)
The end of the first eighteen lessons (20 minutes)
(Revision period)
then
One end of stage exam
End Of Stage Informal Exam (1 hour)

Methodology

The first thing to say about this method is that the basic methodology of delivery is not new in terms of the way the teacher delivers each new concept or word. We are using a tried and tested delivery system which is based on the way you were taught basic speech when you were a child. Most of us learned our basic speech from either our parents or siblings.
We could understand basic speech, make requests and understand demands put to us by those caring for us. This, even before we knew a single grammatical rule or concept.
All we knew was, how to behave, what was right or wrong and how to get what we wanted or needed.

We even knew how to be polite. All this without a single formal lesson or grammar. In fact, we learned these skills simply by copying the words and ideas we heard our parents and siblings say and observing the result negative or positive. Over a four or five year period we learned an enormous amount.

This methodology uses that basic of all learning methods of **listen-repeat-learn, listen-repeat-learn and listen-repeat-learn.** It's simple, basic and easy to administer.
It's as simple as that. If the right concepts or words are introduced in a logical and systematic order then the student begins to understand what gets results and praise from the teacher, whilst sometimes not fully understanding the full meaning of the sentence. Complete understanding in the early stages is not important.

In the early stages a full understanding is not necessary. Things will fall into place naturally as we progress and the student makes the connections himself or herself..

Below is a schematic of this six step principle

1). Introduce new words within a simple sentence giving the translation in the students own language.

2). Ask the student to repeat the sentence, whilst you the teacher speak along with the student **(Tandem Speaking)**, coinciding the teachers speech with the
students speech. Effectively, speaking together.

3). Correcting mistakes the moment they occur.

4). The sentence should be read together from the book.

5). Follow the same procedure and repeat the sentence a second time.

6). Once the lesson has been covered twice and revision has taken place at home and in-class, he or she should be able to recognise the question and answer the question partly from memory. This can only be achieved if the student follows the home study advice given by the teacher. Remember if necessary use the **(Tagging Principle)** to push the students memory.

Positive Reinforcement

At all stages of learning, the student should be given positive reinforcement. This is essential to keep the student motivated.

Notes to the teacher

1). When asking a question during the lesson it is essential that the teacher makes the question sound like a question, using not only the voice but the arms and eyes. This will help the student recognise the basis of what is required as a response. The teacher should be animated.

2). Remember that in the early stages it is most important to always prompt the student when waiting for a response by if necessary; starting the reply so that the student can ***"tag onto"*** what is required. This is called ***"Tagging"***

This acts as a sort of kick-start to an answer and will jog the student's memory. You will quickly notice that the student will then follow-up with the next few words at least if not the rest of the reply. The student will then eventually take control and develop so much familiarity with the question or concept that he or she will be able to answer independently.

3). At first, it isn't necessary for the student to fully understand the question or answer or concept. It is enough at first to be able to respond with the correct response. In the same way as he or she did as a young child.

4). You will notice that as we go through the stages some words are introduced twice. This is necessary when related words are introduced to simply reinforce the relationship of those words.

5). ***"Tagging"*** and ***"Tandem Speaking"*** are both central to this method. Tandem speaking is when both the student and teacher speak together. Tagging is when we offer the first word of an answer to prompt the student's memory. A little like giving a child a push on his bicycle to get him moving.

6). In real life in English, we tend to contract as many words as is possible. Therefore, it's important to introduce those words in the contracted form as early as possible. After all, if our students are going to be able to communicate in the street, they will need to be able to recognise contracted forms used in the street.

Teaching Points

On each teaching page you will notice that after a set of new words or word groups are introduced, there will be a ***"Teaching Point"*** this is there to help you deliver the words and to give you ideas of when and where to expand your questioning and the use of available props. The props needed for that particular section are listed in the teaching point.

Word Introduction

Each section of these books will offer many new words or word groups in a logical and usable order. Usually in sets of two to six words. The words are then put into sentences or questions so as to contextualise each new word. Don't move onto the next set of words until the student can pronounce the word correctly. You will also notice that the translation is given in the students own language so that the student recognizes the meaning.

Grammar Terminology

Although, as already stated, grammar understanding is not important at the beginning. We concentrate on word pronunciation first and the grammar is introduced when needed and relevant.

Within the first stage you will find sections on basic greetings and questions. From the beginning it's important to get the student used to speaking English. You will probably find that the student, regardless of his or her nationality will know some basic greetings in English such as "good morning" or "hello" These words or phrases will have been learned through watching movies or listening to music etc. So, when a student arrives or leaves the class, confidence can start to develop through using and understanding basic greeting terminology.

This should be encouraged and enforced on arriving and leaving. Again, if the student struggles at the beginning just use the ***Tagging*** and ***Tandem Speaking*** techniques mentioned above.

When greeting the student for the first time into the school you can immediately start the process by saying **"good morning"** in English of course or depending on the time of day altering the statement and then explaining the translation in the students own language. Then each time the student arrives for a class repeat the statement until the student begins to accept the statement and responds automatically with a correct response such as "good morning" in reply. Then you can begin to expand on that greeting by introducing such phrases as "how are you today" etc. etc. This will begin to give the student confidence because after he or she makes the statement you respond in a positive way. Always speak with a smile. A happy face is very inviting.

Dictations

Most of the sections have one or more dictations. When delivering dictations you should repeat each section to the student twice, more if needed. You should read the whole dictation back to the student once you have finished delivering it. Then the student should mark the dictation him or herself. The student should then write out a list of the errors made on the sheet provided.

English Idioms & Vocabulary

Lesson One

Each section in this book contains twenty English idioms with explanations. As with the other books in this method the student repeats the idiom until the pronunciation is correct and the meaning is understood.

Where possible the Portuguese equivalent is compared alongside. Each section contains sixty idioms and a short self-test at the end.

Here is the first idiom of six hundred.

Animal Idioms (1)

1).

DOG, WORKED

IDIOM **To work like a dog.**
MEANING **To work very, very much.**
EXAMPLE **The man worked like a dog all his life.**

Question: How hard do you work?
Answer: I work very, very hard, like a dog.

2).

AHEAD, EVERYONE, PACK

IDIOM Ahead of the pack
MEANING To be in front of everyone else in what he or she is doing.
EXAMPLE The product was launched ahead of the competition.

Question: How are your English studies going?
Answer: Very well thank you. I am well ahead of the pack.

3).

ALLEY CAT, ARRIVE

IDIOM She is like an alley cat.
MEANING She stays out very late at night.
EXAMPLE That woman is like an alley cat.

Question: What time did your sister arrive home last night?
Answer: I don't know but she is just like an alley cat.

4).

BAT, BLIND

IDIOM As blind as a bat.
MEANING The person is very blind. Cannot see very well.
EXAMPLE I didn't see it. I must be as blind as a bat.

Question: Did you see that girl walk past the window this morning?
Answer: No, I'm as blind as a bat.

5).

BUSY, BEAVER, GARAGE, AFTERNOON

IDIOM As busy as a beaver
MEANING Means that the person is very, very busy.
EXAMPLE The worker was working like a beaver.

Question: Can you help me to clean my garage this afternoon please?
Answer: No, sorry I'm as busy as a beaver this afternoon. But I can help you tomorrow.

6).

BENT, HIND LEG, STRAIGHT, TRUST

IDIOM As bent as a dogs hind leg.
MEANING Means that the object or idea is not straight.
EXAMPLE His idea was as bent as a dogs back leg.

Question: I wouldn't trust him. He is as bent as a dogs hind leg.
Answer: Me neither. I don't trust him.

7).

DRUNK, SKUNK

IDIOM As drunk as a skunk.
MEANING Means that the person has had too much alcohol to drink.
EXAMPLE The man was as drunk as a skunk when he arrived home.

Question: Have you ever been as drunk as a skunk?
Answer: Yes, Last Friday night.

8).

FAT, PIG, ANIMAL, WEIGHT

IDIOM As fat as a pig.
MEANING Meaning that the person or animal is very fat or over weight. The person has been eating too much.
EXAMPLE The man is as fat as a pig.

Question: Have you always had that beautiful body?
Answer: No, when I was a child I was as fat as a pig.

9).

GENTLE, LAMB, LOVELY

IDIOM As gentle as a lamb.
MEANING The person or animal is very gentle or kind.
EXAMPLE The man was as gentle as a lamb with the baby.

Question: Have you met my new dog? He is as gentle as a lamb with children.
Answer: He is a lovely dog. What's his name?

10).

HUNGRY, WOLF, MOMENT

IDIOM As hungry as a wolf.
MEANING The person is very, very hungry.
EXAMPLE When I arrived home from work, I was as hungry as a wolf.

Question: Are you hungry at the moment?
Answer: Yes, I haven't eaten since 7am this morning. I'm as hungry as a wolf.

Word translations.

Work; Trabalho; Dog; Cão; Ahead; á frente
Pack; Matilha; Everyone; Todos; Else; Mais
Doing; Fazendo; Product; Produto; Launch; Lançamento
Competition; Competiçao; Alley Cat; Gata no cio; Late; Tarde
Night; Noite; Stay; Ficar; Blind; Cego
Bat; Morcego; Busy; Ocupado; Beaver; Castor
Bent; Curva; Hind; Parte de tras; Object; Objeto
Straight; Reto; Drunk; Bebado; Skunk; Gamba
Alcohol; Alcool; Arrived; Chegado; Fat;Gordo
Pig; Porco; Weight; Pesado; Gentle; Gentil
Lamb; Cordeiro; Kind; Amável; Baby; Bebê
Hungry; Com Fome; Wolf; Lobo; In front of; Em Frente

Teaching Point

Practice the new words by repeating them over and over and ask the student to repeat the idiom by using the Tagging principle to prompt the student and then repeat together by using the Tandeming technique until the student can recite independently.

Food Idioms (1)

11).

APPLE, EYE, SPECIAL, DAUGHTER, YOUNGEST

IDIOM **She is the apple of my eye**
MEANING **She is very special to me.**
EXAMPLE **His youngest daughter is the apple of his eye.**

Question: Your daughter is lovely.
Answer: Yes, she is the apple of my eye.

12).

BAD, EGG, KIND

IDIOM **He is a bad egg.**
MEANING **He or she is a bad kind of person.**
EXAMPLE **That man is a bad egg.**

Question: What did you think of her new boyfriend?
Answer: I didn't like him at all. My friend Jane said he is a bad egg.

13).

CHEESE, IMPORTANT, AIRLINE

Idiom **He is a big cheese.**
Meaning **Very important person.**
Example **He is a big cheese in the city.**

Question: Who is that gentleman standing by the door?
Answer: That's Richard Branson. He's a big cheese in the airline business.

14).

BUTTER, BASIS, BASIC

Idiom **It's my bread and butter.**
Meaning **It's the basis of what I am doing.**
Example **The basic needs of my life.**

Question: I can't lose this job. Its my bread and butter.
Answer: Me neither, I hope the company can solve its financial problems.

15).

BACON, BRINGING, DELIVER, ENJOYING

Idiom **Bringing home the bacon.**
Meaning **To earn a living from work done. To deliver on time.**
Example **He always brings home the bacon.**

Question: I'm really enjoying my job at the moment. Its the best feeling in the world, bringing home the bacon. How is your job going?

Answer: Yes, I agree. I'm loving it.

16).

FLATTERING, OF COURSE, HOMEWORK

Idiom **To butter someone up.**
Meaning **To be flattering in order to get one's own way.**
Example **I will have to butter her up to get what I need.**

Question: She wont help me with my homework so I will have to butter her up a little. Can you help me?
Answer: Yes of course. What do you want me to say?

17).

CARROT, STICK, RAISE

Idiom To use a carrot and stick
Meaning To offer a reward for a task to be done.
Example The raise was a carrot and stick for him to get the job done.

Question: He wont do the job for me. He says he wants more money. Do you think a raise will be a carrot and stick for him?
Answer: It depends how much you offer him.

18).

CUCUMBER, CALM, PRESSURE, REACTED

Idiom To be as cool as a cucumber.
Meaning Calm under pressure.
Example He was as cool as a cucumber when telling me.

Question: I can't believe how he reacted this morning. Did you know how good he is?
Answer: Yes, he is as cool as a cucumber.

19).

COUCH, BECOME, LAZY

Idiom He is a couch potato
Meaning To be lazy.
Example He has become a couch potato since he lost his job.

Question: He has become really lazy since he lost his job. Have you got any ideas to get him moving again.
Answer: No, he has always been a couch potato.

20).

CREAM, CROP, AVAILABLE

Idiom It is the cream of the crop.
Meaning He, she or it is the best available.
Example The students are the cream of the crop.

Question: What do you think of my students?
Answer: *They are the cream of the crop and they will do very well in the exams next week.*

Word translations.

Apple; Maçã; Eye; Olho; Youngest; Mais Jovem
Bad; Ruim; Egg; Ovo; Cheese; Queijo
Butter; Manteiga; Bread; Pão; Deliver; Distribuir
Bacon; Bacon; Flattering; Alisador; Carrot; Cenoura
Stick; Vara; Reward; Recompensa; Task; Trabalho
Raise; Lavantar; Job; Trlhoaba; Cool; Fresco
Cucumber; Pepino; Calm; Calma; Pressure; Pressão
Couch; Sofá; Potato; Batata; Lost; Perdido
Cream; Creme; Crop; Colheita; Lazy; Preguiçoso

End of lesson one (Forty five minutes)

It's important at this point to review all of the words and idioms one more time before moving onto lesson number two. Once the student is comfortable then it's safe to move forward.

End of lesson one test

Below you will find a short test which covers the first lesson. This short twenty minute test is meant as a revision and not as a marker for how well the student is progressing.

Tests all the way through these books are for motivational and revision purposes only. People perform differently under exam pressures and we believe that a student's primary aim is to learn a new skill and not to prove his or her worth. So, when giving the tests keep it light. The tests consist of ten questions and a short dictation containing some of the words introduced.

You will also find the answering sheets and answer sheets below. Please feel free to print off as many as needed for each of your students.

End of lesson one dictation

The man was as cool as a cucumber as he walked down the street. He had lost his dog whilst shopping this morning. He always works hard during the week and never fails to bring home the bacon. When he bought his dog as a puppy it was the cream of the crop and it had a black and white face. He lives is in a very poor area and the men living next door were all bad eggs. One of the men had lost his job recently and had become a couch potato.

Ten questions about idioms.
Enter the missing words in the right hand column.

1; As cool as a _______________.;
2; He is a ________ egg.;
3; The __________ of the ________.;
4; I offered him a ______ and stick.;
5; He always brings home the ____________;
6; The students were the __________ of the crop.;
7; I had to butter her ______.;
8; I lost the job that was my bread and ________.;
9; When I arrived home I was as hungry as a _______.;
10; He was a _____ cheese in the city.;

Review the answers on the following page

Once the test is completed do a full review of all the errors and questions the student may have.

It's important to note that each section carries the same introduction and instruction as the last.

Test Answers

1; As cool as a _______________.; Cucumber
2; He is a _______ egg.; Bad
3; The _________ of the _______.;Cream, Crop
4; I offered him a ______ and stick.; Carrot
5; He always brings home the ___________; Bacon
6; The students were the _________ of the crop.; Cream
7; I had to butter her _____.; Up
8; I lost the job that was my bread and _______.; Butter
9; When I arrived home I was as hungry as a ______.; Wolf
10; He was a _____ cheese in the city.; Big

Lesson Two

Food Idioms (2)

21).

HUMBLE PIE, PROVED, ADMIT

Idiom **To eat humble pie**
Meaning **Means to admit one's mistakes.**
Example **He had to eat humble pie when he was proved to be wrong.**

Question: I got the situation completely wrong and I had to admit defeat. Have you ever had to eat humble pie?
Answer: Yes, I can be very embarrassing.

22).

SPEND, CASH

Idiom **To have one's cake and eat it.**
Meaning **You can't have it and spend it at the same time.**
Example **You can't have your cake and eat it. Save your money.**

Question: I bought a new car this morning, but I wish I hadn't spent so much money. Can you lend me some cash until Friday?
Answer: No, you can't have your cake and eat it.

23).

PASSED, DRIVING, TEST, MOUTH

Idiom **To eat your words.**
Meaning **You must take something back after you have said it.**
Example **He made me eat my words.**

Question: I told my friend he wouldn't pass his driving test this morning, but he passed easily. Have you ever had to eat your words?
Answer: You really should think before you open your mouth in the future.

24).

ENCOURAGE, EGGED, WINDOW, PLAYING

Idiom **To egg someone on.**
Meaning **To encourage someone to do something**
Example **The boy egged him on to do it.**

Question: He broke that window with a ball this morning. Were you playing football with him?
Answer: Yes, I'm sorry it was my fault. I was egging him on.

25).

FINGER, PIES, INVOLVED, ACTIVITIES

Idiom **To have a finger in many pies.**
Meaning **He is involved in lots of activities.**
Example **That man has his finger in too many pies.**

Question: Are you very busy at the moment?
Answer: Yes, I have my finger in too many pies at the moment.

26).

BEANS, ENERGY, HEALTHY

Idiom **To be full of beans.**
Meaning **The children are full of energy.**
Example **You are full of beans this morning.**

Question: Do you feel healthy at the moment?
Answer: Yes, I'm full of beans today.

27).

GRAVY, TRAIN, PROFITABLE, JUMPED

Idiom **The gravy train.**
Meaning **Something profitable to be involved in.**
Example **He jumped onto the gravy train at the right time.**

Question: Why don't you try selling second hand phones too to make some extra money?
Answer: No, there are too many people already on that gravy train.

28).

HALF-BAKED, PROPERTY, THROUGH

Idiom **A half-baked idea.**
Meaning **Something that is not properly thought through.**
Example **I never follow a half-baked idea.**

Question: Do you want to go into business with me selling umbrellas in Africa?
Answer: No, its a half-baked idea.

29).

PLATTER, SILVER, RECEIVED

Idiom **To hand something on a silver platter.**
Meaning **Something received in an easy way.**
Example **He received his fortune on a silver platter.**

Question: How did he make all that money?
Answer: He was handed it on a silver platter by his father.

30).

CRACK, NUT, BOSS, INVOLVED

Idiom **It is a hard nut to crack.**
Meaning **A difficult problem to solve.**
Example **My boss is a hard nut to crack.**

Question: I would like to go into business making telephones. Would you like to be involved?
Answer: No, its a hard nut to crack.

Word table with translations.

Humble Humilde Train Trem Silver Prata
Pie Torta Profit Lucro Platter Prato
Spend Pagar Jumped Salto Recieved Receber
Money Dinheiro Half Metade Hard Duro
Encourage Encorajar Baked Cozer Nut Noz
Finger Dedo Properly Corretamente Crack Fender
Lots Muito Thought Pensamento Problem Problema
Beans Feijóes Through Através Boss Chefe
Energy Energia Follow Seguir Something Alguma Coisa
Gravy Molho de carne Idea Idéia Difficult Dificil

Teaching Point

Practice the new words by repeating them over and over and ask the student to repeat the idioms by using the Tagging principle to prompt the student and then repeat together by using the Tandeming technique until the student can recite independently.

Animal Idioms (2)

31).

ACT, APE, BEHAVE

Idiom **Act like an ape**
Meaning **To behave badly**
Example **He was acting like an ape.**

Question: Why did you act like an ape last night?
Answer: Sorry, I had too much to drink.

32).

TONGUE, UNABLE

Idiom **The cat has your tongue**
Meaning **Unable to say anything.**
Example **Has the cat got your tongue.**

Question: Can you ask him why he didn't speak up at the meeting?
Answer: I already asked him if the cat has got his tongue.

33).

BARK, WORSE, BITE, ACTIONS

Idiom **Her bark is worse than her bite.**
Meaning **Someone's words are worse than her actions**
Example **Don't worry his bark is worse than his bite**

Question: Why did she speak to me like that this morning?
Answer: Don't worry, her bite is worse than her bite.

34).

WRONG, HORSE, INVEST, RESEARCH

Idiom **To bet on the wrong horse.**
Meaning **To misread future events.**
Example **I lost all my money. I bet on the wrong horse.**

Question: Did you decide which business to invest in?
Answer: No not yet. I don't want to bet on the wrong horse. I need to do a little more research first.

35).

BULL, CHINA, APPROACHED

Idiom **Like a bull in a china shop.**
Meaning **A person with no tact.**
Example **He approached the problem like a bull in a china shop.**

Question: Do you think you should have been so rude to that man?
Answer: I'm sorry, I have always been like a bull in a china shop.

36).

CATNAP

Idiom **To take a catnap.**
Meaning **To have a very short sleep.**
Example **I'm going to take a catnap while I have time.**

Question: I'm very tired do you mind if I rest?
Answer: No fine. Have a catnap.

37).

MIDSTREAM, HORSES, CHANGE, DECISION

Idiom **To change horses in midstream.**
Meaning **To change your plans halfway through a plan.**
Example **He changed horses midstream.**

Question: I thought I had made the right decision. But I think I'm going to change horses in midstream. Do you mind?
Answer: No I don't.

38).

COPYCAT, IDEAS, NOTICE, ANSWERS

Idiom **He is a copycat.**
Meaning **To copy another person's words, ideas or work.**
Example **Don't be a copycat.**

Question: Did you notice the guy sitting next to me in the exam?
Answer: Yes, he was coping your answers. Copycat!

39).

CRY, WOLF, BELIEVES, CRIED

Idiom **To cry wolf.**
Meaning **To give a false warning.**
Example **She cried wolf, now no one believes her.**

Question: If he hadn't told me he was in trouble twice already this week I might have believed him.
Answer: Yes, its stupid to cry wolf.

40).

TROUBLE, NOSEY, CONCERNED, CURIOSITY, RUDE, KILLED

Idiom **Curiosity killed the cat.**
Meaning **To be nosey. To be concerned about someone else's business.**
Example **She got into deep trouble being too curious. You know what they say. Curiosity killed the cat.**

Question: Don't ask so many questions its rude. Hasn't anyone ever told you that curiosity killed the cat.
Answer: Yes, but I need to know where we are going.

Word translations.

Act Ato Horse Calvalo Wolf Lobo
Ape Macaco Misread Ler Mal Cried Grito
Behave Comortar-se Bet Aposta Curiosity Curiosidade
Tongue Lingua Bull Touro Killed Assassinado
Cat Gato China Porcelana Business Negócio
Unable Incapaz Shop Loja Trouble Problemo
Bark Casca Nap Dornir She Ela
Bite Morder Midstream Corrente dum Rio Concern Preocupação
Plan Plano FALSE Falso Deep Profundo
Copy Cópia Warning Alarme Else Outro

End of lesson two (Forty five minutes)

It's important at this point to review all of the words and idioms one more time before moving onto lesson number three. Once the student is comfortable then it's safe to move forward.

End of lesson two test

Below you will find a short test which covers the second lesson. This short twenty minute test is meant as a revision and not as a marker for how well the student is progressing.

Tests all the way through these books are for motivational and revision purposes only. People perform differently under exam pressures and we believe that a student's primary aim is to learn a new skill and not to prove his or her worth. So, when giving the tests keep it light. The tests consist of ten questions and a short dictation containing some of the words introduced.

You will also find the answering sheets and answer sheets below. Please feel free to print off as many as needed for each student.

End of lesson two dictation

I had to eat my words today after I had been feeling full of beans because I think I had had my finger in too many pies. I thought I had jumped on the gravy train but actually I had been handed my business on a silver platter. In the end, the idea turned out to be a half-baked idea. I told him not to be a copycat and that he was probably barking up the wrong tree. I had to eat my words after approaching the idea like a bull in a china shop.

Ten questions about idioms.
Enter the missing words in the right hand column.

1 He had to eat _____________ pie.
2 You know what they say. Curiosity killed the __
3 I told him not to act like an ______.
4 He was _____ of beans all day.
5 Has the cat got your ______.
6 He was handed it on a ______ platter.
7 Gravy ________
8 You can't have your ____ and eat it.
9 It was a ____ baked idea.
10 He had too many ____ in too many pies.

The answers are on the following page.

Now Review the answers

Test Answers

1 He had to eat _____________ pie. Humble
2 You know what they say. Curiosity killed the __ Cat
3 I told him not to act like an ______. Ape
4 He was _____ of beans all day. Full
5 Has the cat got your ______. Tongue
6 He was handed it on a ______ platter. Silver
7 Gravy ________ Train
8 You can't have your ____ and eat it. Cake
9 It was a ____ baked idea. Half
10 He had too many ____ in too many pies. Fingers

Lesson Three

Food Idioms (3)

41).

FACE, ONES, JUDGEMENT

Idiom **To have egg on one's face**
Meaning **To be embarrassed**
Example **He made a bad judgement. Now he has egg on his face.**

Question: I really shouldn't have told her should I?
Answer: No, now we all have egg on our faces.

42).

SAUCE, DRINKING

Idiom **To hit the sauce**
Meaning **To start drinking alcohol.**
Example **He got very depressed and so hit the sauce.**

Question: Are we going out on Friday night?
Answer: Yes, can't wait to hit the sauce.

43).

CONTRAVERSIAL, FORGET

Idiom **It's a hot potato.**
Meaning **A controversial subject**
Example **This subject is a hot potato.**
Question: I don't really want to comment yet, do you?
Answer: No, lets forget it. Its a hot potato.

44).

NUTSHELL, SUM

Idiom **In a nutshell**
Meaning **To speak briefly about something. To sum up an idea.**
Example **In a nutshell it's a bad idea.**

Question: What do you think about your new neighbours?
Answer: Well, in a nutshell, they haven't introduced themselves yet and its been two months since they moved in.

45).

SOUP. SERIOUS, TROUBLE, BANKRUPTCY

Idiom **In the soup.**
Meaning **To be in serious trouble**
Example **He landed himself in the soup.**

Question: How do you feel about your brothers financial problems?
Answer: He is really in the soup at the moment. He may have to declare bankruptcy.

46).

WATERMELON, MOUTH, BADLY, HUNGRY

Idiom To make your mouth water.
Meaning **A look or smell that makes you want something badly.**
Example **That smell is making my mouth water. Now I'm hungry.**

Question: Do you want some cool watermelon?
Answer: Yes please, my mouth is watering.

47).

NUTTY, FRUIT CAKE

Idiom Nutty as a fruit cake.
Meaning **To be a little crazy.**
Example **That man is as nutty as a fruit cake**

Question: Do you think she is OK.
Answer: No, I think she is as nutty as a fruitcake.

48).

STUPID, CRAZY, COMPLETE

Idiom **He is a nut.**
Meaning **To be stupid or a little crazy.**
Example **Don't follow him he is a nut.**

Question: Would you employ her?
Answer: No way. She is a complete nut.

49).

FRYING PAN, WORSE, FAVOURITE

Idiom **Out of the frying pan and into the fire.**
Meaning **To make a problem worse than it already was.**
Example **He went from the frying pan and into the fire.**

Question: Lets put our last ten pounds on the favourite horse at the 3pm race at Kempton Park. What do you're. think?
Answer: Are you crazy. Don't gamble, its like going from the frying pan to the fire.

50).

LUNCH, REALLY

Idiom **Out to lunch.**
Meaning **To be a little crazy.**
Example **We can't really trust her with those children because she is a little out to lunch.**

Question: She wasn't listening to what I was saying was she?
Answer: No, that woman seems out to lunch.

Word translations.

Face Face Controversial Controverso Follow Seguir
Embarrassed Embaraçado Soup Sopa Fry Fritar
Judgement Julgamento Serious Sério Pan Panela
Hit Bater Land Terra Worse Pior
Sauce Molho Mouth Boca Already Já
Drink Bebida Water Agua Fire Fogo
Depressed Deprimido Hungry Com Fome Lunch Almoço
Hot Quente Cake Bolo Trust Esperança
Subject Sujeito Fruit Frutas Himself se
Briefly Breve Crazy Louco Man Homan

Teaching Point

Practice the new words by repeating them over and over and ask the student to repeat the idiom by using the Tagging principle to prompt the student and then repeat together by using the Tandeming technique until the student can recite independently.

Animal Idioms (3)

51).

DARK HORSE

Idiom **He is a dark horse.**
Meaning **Someone who is little known to you.**
Example **Don't trust him he is a dark horse.**

Question: Do you think he is OK?
Answer: No, I think he is a dark horse.

52).

REALLY, HURT, SELFISH, GAINS, HATE

Idiom **Dog eat dog**
Meaning **Ready to hurt others to make selfish gains.**
Example **In this tech world, it's dog eat dog**

Question: I hate this business. Don't you?
Answer: Yes, life is dog eat dog these days.

53).

DONKEY´S

Idiom **For donkey's years.**
Meaning **Meaning for many years.**
Example **I've known him for donkey's years.**

Question: How long have you lived in Brazil?
Answer: For donkeys years.

54).

DUMB, BUNNY, BELIEVES

Idiom To be a dumb bunny.
Meaning **Someone who is gullible. Believes anything she is told.**
Example **She is a bit of a dumb bunny.**

Question: Do you think she could do the job?
Answer: No, to be honest she seems a dumb bunny.

55).

EAGER, BEAVER, ENTHUSIASTIC

Idiom **An eager beaver.**
Meaning **Someone who is eager to get things done.**
Example **Don't be such an eager beaver. Think first.**

Question: He seems very enthusiastic doesn't he?
Answer: Yes, a real eager beaver.

56).

HUNGRY

Idiom	**To eat like a horse.**
Meaning	**He or she eats a lot of food.**
Example	**I was so hungry I ate like a horse.**

Question: Are you hungry at the moment?
Answer: Yes, I could eat a horse.

57).

EVENTUALLY, EVERYDAY

Idiom	**Every dog has his day.**
Meaning	**Everyone's day comes eventually.**
Example	**Don't worry, every dog has his day eventually.**

Question: I'm glad he got his visa finally, are you?
Answer: Yes, well every dog has his day.

58).

ARROGANTLY, HIGH, HORSE, UPSET

Idiom	**To get on one's high horse.**
Meaning	**To behave arrogantly.**
Example	**OK don't get on your high horse. I agree with you.**

Question: He got very upset with me this morning. Do you know what the problem was?
Answer: No, don't worry. He always gets on his high horse.

59).

APE, SOMETHING, LADDERED, STOCKINGS

Idiom	**To go ape about something.**
Meaning	**To go crazy or excited about something.**
Example	**Don't go ape about it.**

Question: What was wrong with her this morning?
Answer: I don't know. She just went ape when I told her that her stockings were laddered.

60).

BULLS EYE, ACCURATE

Idiom	**To hit the bulls eye.**
Meaning	**To be accurate about something. To the point.**
Example	**He really hit the bulls eye with his comments.**

Question: Do you think I should tell him about the bad workmanship?
Answer: Yes, you hit the bulls eye when you said his work is poor.

End of lesson three (Forty minutes)

Teaching Point

It's important at this point to review all of the words and idioms one more time before moving onto section two. Once the student is comfortable then it's safe to move forward.

Word translations.

Dark Escuro Known Conhecido Eat Comer
Selfish Egoista Gain Ganho Donkey Burro
Dumb Estupido Rabbit Coelho Bunny Coelho
Gullible Crédulo Bit Pouco Eager Impaciente
Beaver Castor Like Gostar Food Comida
High Alto Bull Touro Accurate Preciso
Point Ponto Comment Contentário Get Receber

End of lesson three test

Below you will find a short test which covers the third lesson. This short twenty minute test is meant as a revision and not as a marker for how well the student is progressing.

Tests all the way through these books are for motivational and revision purposes only. People perform differently under exam pressures and we believe that a student's primary aim is to learn a new skill and not to prove his or her worth. So, when giving the tests keep it light. The tests consist of ten yes or no questions and a short dictation containing some of the words introduced.

You will also find the answering sheets below. Please feel free to print off as many as needed for each student.

End of section dictation.

I knew him for donkey's years but he was always a dark horse. In this life it is dog eat dog so I never get on my high horse and become an eager beaver about anything. I arrived home very hungry, in fact as hungry as a horse. My dinner wasn't ready so I got on my high horse and went a little ape with her. When she said I was being rude she hit the bulls eye.

Ten questions about idioms.
Enter the missing words in the right hand column.

1 He got on his ______ horse about it.
2 I always eat like a __________
3 You know every ____ has his day
4 Don't go ______ about it. Everything will be ok.
5 I have known him for ______ years.
6 She is a bit of a ______ bunny.
7 Don't be such an _______ beaver.
8 Don't trust him he is a dark _____.
9 This modern world is ____ eat ____.
10 She hit the bulls ____ when she said it.

Review the test answers on the following page

Test Answers

1	He got on his ______ horse about it.	High
2	I always eat like a __________.	Horse
3	You know every ____ has his day.	Dog
4	Don't go ______ about it. Everything will be OK.	Ape
5	I have known him for ______ years.	Donkey's
6	She is a bit of a ______ bunny.	Dumb
7	Don't be such an _______ beaver.	Eager
8	Don't trust him he is a dark _____.	Horse
9	This modern world is ____ eat ____.	Dog Dog
10	She hit the bulls ____ when she said it.	Eye

Lesson Four

Each lesson in this e-book contains twenty English idioms with explanations. As with the other e-books in this method the student repeats the idiom until the pronunciation is correct and the meaning is understood. Where possible the Portuguese equivalent is compared alongside. Each e-book contains sixty idioms and a short self-test at the end.

Work Idioms (1)

61).

ACROSS, BOARD, INCLUDE, CHANGES

Idiom **Across the board.**
Meaning **To include everyone and everything.**
Example **I am making changes across the board**

Question: What does across the board mean?
Possible Answer: It means to include everything and or everyone.

62).

LOSS, OPPOSITE, LOSE, PROFIT, BUSINESS

Idiom **Working at a loss**
Meaning **The opposite to making a profit. To lose money**
Example **My business was making a loss.**

Question: Would you be happy running a business at a loss?
Possible Answer: No of course not. A business needs to make a profit.

63).

BAIL, COMPANY, TROUBLE, DEFAULT

Idiom **To bail out a company.**
Meaning **A bank may bail out a company when it's in trouble.**
Example **The EU had to bail out Greece after it defaulted on its loans.**

Question: What does to bail out mean?
Possible Answer: It means to pay money to get someone or something out of trouble.

64).

BETWEEN, DURING, USUALLY

Idiom **Banking hours**
Meaning **Usually doing business between 9am and 4pm**
Example **Our office is open during banking hours.**
Question: What time does your bank close?
Possible Answer: I think it closes at 4pm.

65).

PARK, FIGURE, ESTIMATE

Idiom **A ball park figure.**
Meaning **It's an estimate of the cost.**
Example **I can give you a ball park figure of the costs.**

Question: Can you give me a ball park figure of how much you want to sell your car for?
Possible Answer: Yes, I want about two thousand pounds for it.

66).

GUN, IMPORTANT, FIELD

Idiom **A big gun**
Meaning **Someone important in the business world.**
Example **He is one of the big guns in his field of work.**

Question: Who was that guy I saw at the school yesterday?
Possible Answer: It was one of the company big guns.**67).**

FELL, MARKET, DEMAND, DISAPPEARED, PRODUCT

Idiom **The bottom fell out of the market.**
Meaning **The demand has disappeared.**
Example **The bottom has fallen out of the market for this product.**

Question: Is your business still growing?
Possible Answer: No, we stopped trading and closed our shop because the bottom fell of the widget business.

68).

WIG

Idiom	**Big wig.**
Meaning	**An important person.**
Example	**Here comes the big wigs. We had better work hard.**

Question: How many managers are there at your place of work?
Possible Answer: There are too many at the moment. They all think they are big wigs.

69).

BASIS, DISCUSSION, EXPENSIVE

Idiom	**The bottom line is this.**
Meaning	**The basis of our discussions.**
Example	**The bottom line is that it's too expensive.**

Question: What do you think about what happened this morning at work?
Possible Answer: The bottom line is that I don't really care anymore I just quit.

70).

ECONOMY, REACHED, PERFORMANCE, INFLATION

Idiom	**To bottom out.**
Meaning	**An economy has reached the bottom of it's performance.**
Example	**We think inflation has bottomed out for the present time.**

Question: What do you think about the state of the British economy at the moment?
Possible Answer: I am hoping that the unemployment figures have bottomed out and the country starts to recover soon.

Word table with translations

Across Através de Demand Procura
Board Conselho Disappeared Desaparecido
Include Incluir Wig Chinó
Bail Concha Better Melhor
Defaulted Negligência Expensive Dispendioso
Loan Emprestar Discussion Discussão
Estimate Estimativa Reach Alcançar
Figure Imaginar Bottom Fundo
Gun Pistola Present Apresentar

Teaching Point

Practice the new words by repeating them over and over and ask the student to repeat the idiom by using the Tagging principle to prompt the student and then repeat together by using the Tandeming technique until the student can recite independently.

Work Idioms (2)

71).

VALUE, CHECKING, TRUST, EMPLOYED

Idiom **On face value.**
Meaning **To trust something or someone without checking.**
Example **I employed him on face value.**

Question: What do you think of the new manager?
Possible Answer: All I can do is take him on face value and see what he is like as we get to know him.

72).

FIGURE, UNDERSTAND

Idiom **To figure something out.**
Meaning **To try and understand something.**
Example **I am trying to figure the problem out.**

Question: Can you help me figure out what's going on?
Possible Answer: I would, but I don't know where to start.

73).

FAIR, JUSTICE

Idiom **Fair play**
Meaning **Meaning to be fair and give justice to something.**
Example **Well, fair play to him. He was right after all.**
Question: What do you think about downloading music for free from the internet?
Possible Answer: I guess fair play to people if they get away with it. But its definitely illegal.

74).

FIT, BILL

Idiom **To fit the bill.**
Meaning **It´s just what we needed or were looking for.**
Example **I think we will buy it because it fits the bill.**

Question: What do you think about the new teacher?
Possible Answer: Well, I think he really fits the bill here.

75).

GAIN, GROUND, THOUGHT, OBVIOUSLY

Idiom **To gain ground.**
Meaning **To move forward with something.**
Example **I thought we were gaining ground. But obviously not.**

Question: Is your fathers car business doing well?
Possible Answer: Yes, he seems to be gaining ground on the competition.

76).

DISCUSSED

Idiom To give someone the green light.
Meaning **To say yes let's do it.**
Example **I gave him the green light after we discussed it.**

Question: Are you still going to go to Australia to live?
Possible Answer: Yes, I'm just waiting for the green light from immigration.

77).

BREAK, OPPORTUNITY, PROBLEM

Idiom **To get a break.**
Meaning **To have an opportunity.**
Example **We need to get a break with this problem**

Question: Trying to start a new business is very difficult. Do you agree?
Possible Answer: Yes, you just need a lucky break.

78).

CHANCE, MISTAKE

Idiom **Give me a break.**
Meaning **To give someone a chance to do something.**
Example **OK, I made a mistake. But give me a break.**

Question: If I needed a job, would you give me a break?
Possible Answer: Yes, of course I would if I needed help in my business.

79).

STARTED

Idiom **To get it off the ground.**
Meaning **To get something started for the first time.**
Example **We need to get this business off the ground.**

Question: I thought you said you were going to start a new business. How is it going?
Possible Answer: I am finding it difficult to get it off the ground. I need more money.

80).

RUNNING

Idiom **Off and running.**
Meaning **Something that has started.**
Example **We are off and running.**

Question: What time does the London Marathon start this morning?
Possible Answer: I believe they are off and running now.

Word translations.

Value Valor Light Claro Off ir embora
Checking Guarda de Objetos Opportunity Oportunidade
Employed Usar Break Pausa
Fair Justo Problem Problema
Justice Equidade Started Começar
Bill Conta Running Corrida
Needed Precisar de Play Jogar
Gain Ganhar Because Porque
Ground Terra Forward á Frente

End of lesson four (Forty minutes)

It's important at this point to review all of the words and idioms one more time before moving onto lesson number five. Once the student is comfortable then it's safe to move forward.

End of lesson four test

Below you will find a short test which covers the lesson above. This short twenty minute test is meant as a revision and not as a marker for how well the student is progressing.

Tests all the way through this book are for motivational and revision purposes only. People perform differently under exam pressures and we believe that a student's primary aim is to learn a new skill and not to prove his or her worth. So, when giving the tests keep it light. The tests consist of ten questions and a short dictation containing some of the words introduced.

You will also find the answering sheets and answer sheets below. Please feel free to print off as many as needed for each of your students.

End of lesson four dictation

We started our new business last month and it was a relief to get it off the ground. For the first few months we expect to be running at a loss. When I spoke to my bank manager he had a doubt whether my business would work, but I convinced him that if he gave us the green light to start we would be off and running in no time at all. My business partner was a big wig in the banking industry and so he knew we were onto a winner. We expect to be making a small profit within six months of being up and running. We are confident that our products fit the bill and that sales will eventually be massive.

Ten questions about idioms.
Enter the missing words in the right hand column.

1 Across the __________.
2 __________ at a loss.
3 A ________ out.
4 Banking _______.
5 ______ me a break.
6 He gave us the green _______.
7 He is a ______ wig in the business world.
8 He gave us a ball _______ figure.
9 We had to take it on face _______.
10 The new employee really fits ____ ____.

Review the answers on the next page

Test Answers

1	Board
2	Working
3	Bail
4	Hours
5	Give
6	Light
7	Big
8	Park
9	Value
10	The, Bill

Lesson Five

Each section in this e-book contains twenty English idioms with explanations. As with the other e-books in this method the student repeats the idiom until the pronunciation is correct and the meaning is understood. Where possible the Portuguese equivalent is compared alongside. Each section contains sixty idioms and a short self-test at the end.

Work Idioms (2)

81).

WRITING

Idiom **In black and White**
Meaning **I need it in writing.**
Example **Before I agree to anything I want to see it in black and White.**

Question: Do you always insist on a contract before you make agreements?
Possible Answer: Yes, I never do anything unless its in black and white.

82).

THROUGH, PLANNED, REALLY

Idiom **To go through with it.**
Meaning **To do something as planned.**
Example **Are you really going to go through with it?**

Question: Are you still going to change jobs?
Possible Answer: I am still thinking about whether to go through with it.

83).

SELL, TECHNIQUES

Idiom **It was a hard sell.**
Meaning **Someone trying to sell something to you face to face.**
Example **I don´t like hard sell techniques.**

Question: I hate door to door salesmen. Don't you?
Possible Answer: Yes, I do. I hate the hard sell.

84).

CHARGE, RESPONSIBLE, MANAGER, PROJECT

Idiom **In charge of.**
Meaning **Meaning to be responsible for something.**
Example **The manager is in charge of the project.**

Question: Who is in charge of this school?
Possible Answer: Rose is the Managing Director and owner.

85).

ROLL, ACCOUNT, SOLVE

Idiom **Heads will roll.**
Meaning **People will be held to account.**
Example **If we don´t solve this problem heads will roll.**

Question: What do you think should happen to John now we know he has been found guilty of corruption?
Possible Answer: Well, I'm not sure but heads will roll.

86).

SUPPLY, AROUND

Idiom **In short supply.**
Meaning **Not many of them around.**
Example **Good workers are in short supply.**

Question: I have been looking for a book explaining Chinese grammar. Do you know where can get one.
Possible Answer: I don't know. But they are in short supply.

87).

STOCK, PRODUCTS, SALE, MOMENT

Idiom **To have in stock.**
Meaning **To have the products available for sale.**
Example **We have a lot of them in stock at the moment.**

Question: Do you know if they have the new iPhone in stock yet?
Possible Answer: Yes, I think they have them in stock now, but they are very expensive.

88).

MAINTAIN, ACCOUNTS, RESPONSIBLE

Idiom **To keep the books.**
Meaning **To maintain your accounts.**
Example **He is the person responsible for keeping the books.**

Question: Who keeps the books for your business?
Possible Answer: We have a professional accounting company to take care of our legal responsibilities.

89).

TRACK, AWARE, ACTIVITIES

Idiom **To keep track.**
Meaning **To be aware of something.**
Example **I have been keeping track of your activities.**

Question: Do you have a good system in place to keep track of all the books you have?
Possible Answer: Yes, I use a card index filing system.

90).

KICKBACK, ILLEGAL, CORRUPTLY, CONTACT

Idiom A kickback.
Meaning **An illegal payment made to someone corruptly.**
Example **He received a kickback after signing the contract.**

Question: What do you think about corruption in the police?
Possible Answer: Any officer that takes a kickback should be fired and prosecuted.

Word table with translations.

Writing Escrita Heads Cabeças Products Produtos
Before Antes People Pessoas Available Disponivel
Through Através Account Cálculo Moment Momento
Really Realamente Roll Enrolar Maintain Manter
Hard Dificil Short Curto Illegal Ilegal
Sell Vender Supply Provisão Payment Pagamento
Techniques Téchnica Around Em torno Corruptly Corruptamente
Meaning Significado Good Bom Received Receber
Responsible Responsável Workers Trabalhador Signing Assinatura
Project Projeto Stock Armazenar Contract Contrato

Teaching Point

Practice the new words by repeating them over and over and ask the student to repeat the idioms by using the Tagging principle to prompt the student and then repeat together by using the Tandeming technique until the student can recite independently.

Work Idioms (3)

91).

HARD

Idiom **Make a go of it.**
Meaning **To try hard to do something.**
Example **I am going to make a real go of it.**

Question: I'm thinking of starting a file sharing business on the internet. What do you think?
Possible Answer: Well I hope can make a go of it. Others have failed.

92).

BUSINESS, DETERMINED

Idiom **To mean business.**
Meaning **To be determined about something.**
Example **He really means business.**

Question: My friend next door said he is going to start a business competing with mine. Do you think he means business.
Possible Answer: Maybe, he does. Maybe he doesn't.

93).

NUMBER, CRUNCH, ACCOUNTING, CONTRACT

Idiom **He is a number cruncher.**
Meaning **Someone who Works with numbers. Usually accounting.**
Example **We need to do some number crunching before we sign the contract.**

Question: What do you do for a job?
Possible Answer: I'm a number cruncher of a local business.

94).

CLOSE, BY

Idiom **To have on hand.**
Meaning **Means to have something close by.**
Example **Wait I have it at hand. It´s just on my desk.**

Question: Do you have that book with you I wanted to borrow?
Possible Answer: Yes, I have it on hand. Let me know when you need it.

95).

BLOCK, POSSIBLY, ACTION

Idiom **Head on the block.**
Meaning **To be possibly in trouble for an action.**
Example **It´s your head on the block if anything goes wrong.**

Question: If it all goes wrong, you know its your head on the block. Do you realise that?
Possible Answer: Yes I know, I hope it doesn't all go wrong.

96).

PIECE, ACTION

Idiom **A piece of the action.**
Meaning **To take part in something good.**
Example **I want a piece of the action with this deal.**

Question: I'm going to start a new business. Do you want a piece of the action?
Possible Answer: Yes, but how much will I need to invest?

97).

RECEIVE, PAY-OFF, LOSING, JOB

Idiom **Receive a pay-off.**
Meaning **To receive money usually after losing your job.**
Example **How much did you receive for your pay-off?**

Question: I have just lost my job, but they gave me a play-off.
Possible Answer: **OK** great. How much did you get?

98).

RUN, SHORT, PRODUCT

Idiom **To run short.**
Meaning **To be short on products.**
Example **We are running short of pencils. We should buy more.**

Question: Do we have enough stage eight books for the new students.
Possible Answer: Yes I think so. I will let you know if we run short.

99).

NOSEDIVE, DECREASE, RECESSION

Idiom **To take a nosedive.**
Meaning **To decrease.**
Example **The business took a nose dive during the recession.**

Question: How is your dads new business doing?
Possible Answer: He was doing ok. But recently its taken a nosedive.

100).

SADDLED, DEBT, OWE

Idiom Saddled with debt.
Meaning **To have a lot of debt. Owe too much money.**
Example **The business is saddled with debt. It´s not a good buy.**

Question: Since I lost my job I have been saddled with debt.
Possible Answer: Its not much fun being unemployed.

Word translations.

Try Tentar Block Bloquear Decrease Diminuir
Real Realmente Trouble Problema Recession Recessão
Determined Determinado Action Ação Saddle
Something Alguma Coisa Wrong Errado Debt Divida
Crunch Triturar Piece parte Owe Dever
Number Numero LosingPerder Idea Ideia
Usually Usualmente Product Produto
Accounting Contabilidade Short Breve
Sign Assinar Nose Nariz
Close Fechar Dive Mergulho

End of lesson five (Forty minutes)

It's important at this point to review all of the words and idioms one more time before moving onto lesson number six. Once the student is comfortable then it's safe to move forward.

End of lesson five test

Below you will find a short test which covers the fifth lesson. This short twenty minute test is meant as a revision and not as a marker for how well the student is progressing.

Tests all the way through these books are for motivational and revision purposes only. People perform differently under exam pressures and we believe that a student's primary aim is to learn a new skill and not to prove his or her worth. So, when giving the tests keep it light.

The tests consist of ten questions and a short dictation containing some of the words introduced.

You will also find the answering sheets and answer sheets below. Please feel free to print off as many as needed for each student.

End of lesson five dictation

He asked me to put it in black and white before we go through with the deal. After going through the hard sell, the salesman received a kickback as well as his commission. Luckily, his wife was a number cruncher at work and understood that her husband´s head was on the block if found out. Before the opportunity came along they had been saddled with debt. He had been in charge of a company that had not kept track of its finances.

Ten questions about idioms.
Enter the missing words in the right hand column.

1 We didn't go through with _____.
2 He was in _______ of a very large company.
3 It was difficult to _____ track of the finances.
4 We decided to ______ through ____ it.
5 He received a large _____ off.
6 We received a _____ of the action.
7 The Family was _______ with debt.
8 His wife is a number ______ at work.
9 We have many of those products in ____.
10 He really meant _____ and went through with the deal.

Review the answers on the following page

Test Answers

1	It
2	Charge
3	Keep
4	Go, With
5	Pay
6	Piece
7	Saddled
8	Cruncher
9	Stock
10	Business

Lesson Six

Each section in this section contains twenty English idioms with explanations. As with the other sections in this method the student repeats the idiom until the pronunciation is correct and the meaning is understood. Where possible the Portuguese equivalent is compared alongside. Each section contains sixty idioms and a short self-test at the end.

Random Idioms (1)

101).

CAKES, QUICKLY, EASY

Idiom	**To sell like hot cakes.**
Meaning	**Easy to sell. To sell quickly.**
Example	**My books sold like hot cakes.**

Question: We are selling our old used books of at half price. Would you like any?
Possible Answer: If there any left at the end of the month I will buy some. But I hear they are selling like hot cakes.

102).

NOTHING

Idiom	**Sold Out.**
Meaning	**To have nothing left.**
Example	**We sold out very quickly. Everything has now gone.**

Question: Are the books sold out?
Possible Answer: No, there are quite a few left.

103).

IRON, STRIKE, OPPORTUNITY, OTHERWISE

Idiom	**To strike while the iron is hot.**
Meaning	**To take advantage of an opportunity while it´s available.**
Example	**You have to strike while the iron is hot otherwise you will miss out.**

Question: What does strike while the iron is hot mean?
Possible Answer: It means that you should do it now while the opportunity is still there.

104).

COMPANY, ANOTHER

Idiom	**A take-over.**
Meaning	**When one company takes control of another.**
Example	**The company took over the other company.**

Question: I have heard that the school is being taken over by a much larger company. Is it true?
Possible Answer: Yes, we are all going to be millionaires.

105).

EMPLOY, EMPLOYEES

Idiom	**To take someone on.**
Meaning	**Means to employ someone.**
Example	**We are looking to take on two more employees this year.**

Question: We are looking for a new teacher, do you know anyone who is looking for a job?
Possible Answer: Yes, I would like to be an English teacher, would you consider taking me on?

106).

THROW, PROJECT, PRODUCT

Idiom	**To throw money at something.**
Meaning	**Means to waste money on a project or product.**
Example	**We threw too much money at it and it still isn't right.**

Question: This new business isnt really working. What should do?
Possible Answer: You should stop throwing money at it.

107).

PUBLIC, DECIDED, SCANDAL

Idiom	**To go public.**
Meaning	**To tell the world about something.**
Example	**We decided to go public with the scandal.**

Question: Do you think I should go public with what I know about that politician?
Possible Answer: Yes I do. Its in the public interest.

108).

ENTER, STOCK

Idiom **To go public. (2)**
Meaning **To enter your business onto the stock Market.**
Example **Our business will go public and offer shares.**

Question: My fathers business is doing very well. He is thinking of going public. Would you be interested in buying shares while they are cheap.?
Possible Answer: Yes, if the shares are affordable.

109).

CONSIDER, SERIOUSLY, ISSUES

Idiom **To take stock of something.**
Meaning **Means to consider something seriously.**
Example **You need to take stock of the issues in your life.**

Question: I'm thinking of investing in that new business, what do you think?
Possible Answer: Before you do anything I would take stock of your finances.

110).

COLD, DISCOURAGE, IDEA, THREW

Idiom To throw cold water on it.
Meaning **To discourage something, someone or an idea.**
Example **I told him about my idea but he just threw cold water on it.**

Question: I had a great money making idea. Do you want to join me?
Possible Answer: I would rather throw cold water on your idea. Its a stupid idea.

Word translations.

Hot Quente Control Controle Scandal Escândalo
Cakes Bolos Another Outro Market Mercado
Quickly Rapidamente Throw Jogar Stock Estocar
Sold Vendido Threw Jogou Offer Oferta
Strike Greve Money Dinheiro Shares ações
Iron Ferramenta Project Projeto Seriously Serio
Advantage Vantagem Product Produto Issues Questão
While Durante Public Publico Life Vida
Otherwise De Outro modo World Mundo Cold Frio
Miss Faltar Decided Decidido Discourage Desencorajar

Teaching Point

Practice the new words by repeating them over and over and ask the student to repeat the idiom by using the Tagging principle to prompt the student and then repeat together by using the Tandeming technique until the student can recite independently.

Colour Idioms (2)

111).

TIE, OCCASION, FUNCTION

Idiom **A black tie event.**
Meaning **A formal occasion like a dinner, meeting or a function.**
Example **We are going to a black tie event tonight.**

Question: Would you like to come to the event with me tonight?
Possible Answer: Yes of course. Is it a black tie event?

112).

SHEEP, ODD

Idiom **Black sheep of the Family.**
Meaning **The odd one out.**
Example **She is the black sheep of the Family.**

Question: How many brothers and sisters do you have?
Possible Answer: Just one brother. But he is the black sheep of the family.

113).

PITCH, TURNED

Idiom Its pitch black
Meaning **Very, very dark.**
Example **The room was pitch black before I turned the light on.**

Question: Is it dark outside yet?
Possible Answer: Yes, its pitch black.

114).

HAPPENING, SURPRISE, ARRIVED

Idiom **It came out of the blue.**
Meaning **Something happening by surprise.**
Example **He arrived out of the blue.**

Question: I met an old friend yesterday in a restaurant. He asked me if I wanted to go to Thailand with him. Do you think I should go?
Possible Answer: Yes, of course. When was the last time you were offered a free holiday out of the blue?

115).

SPECIAL, OPINION

Idiom	**A blue eyed boy.**
Meaning	**To be special in someone's opinion.**
Example	**He is the blue eyed boy in this business.**

Question: My brother is the blue eyed boy in our family. Do you know him?
Possible Answer: No, what's his name?

116).

ROYAL, DESCENTE, PRINCE

Idiom	**To have blue blood.**
Meaning	**Of royal descente.**
Example	**The Prince has blue blood.**

Question: Do you think the Royal family really have blue blood?
Possible Answer: No, its just a fixed expression that means that they are different from us.

117).

RIBBON, EVENT, SPECIAL, CERTAINLY

Idiom	**A blue ribbon event.**
Meaning	**A special, first class event. One of a kind.**
Example	**It certainly was a blue ribbon event.**

Question: Would you like to go to a special party with me tonight?
Possible Answer: Yes please. I hear its a blue ribbon event with famous guests.

118).

FEELING, SAD, QUITE

Idiom	**Feeling blue.**
Meaning	**To be sad about something.**
Example	**I woke up this morning feeling quite blue.**

Question: Why are you looking so sad tonight?
Possible Answer: I have been feeling blue all day.

119).

MOON, OCCASIONALLY, NEVER, VISITS

Idiom	**Once in a blue moon.**
Meaning	**Very occasionally or never.**
Example	**He only visits once in a blue moon.**

Question: I'm going to the cinema tonight, do you want to come with me?
Possible Answer: Yes please. I only go to the cinema once in a blue mood.

120).

SAIL, FALSE, DISGUISE, RECOGNISED, PIRATE, SAILING

Idiom **To sail under false colours.**
Meaning **To disguise something so not to be recognised.**
Example **The pirate ship was sailing under false colours.**

Question: In that new movie starring Johnny Depp, a pirate ship sails under false colours and attacks a British war ship. Have you seen it?
Possible Answer: No, what the movie called?

End of lesson Six (Forty minutes)

Teaching Point

It's important at this point to review all of the words and idioms one more time before moving onto e-book three. Once the student is comfortable then it's safe to move forward.

Word translations.

Tie Gravata Odd Estranho Opinion Opinião
Event Evento Pitch Breu Special Especial
Function Função Very Muito Blue Azul
Meeting Reunião Dark Escuro Blood Sangue
Formal Formal Turn Volta Royal Real
Sheep Ovelha Surprise Surpresa Prince Principe
Family Família Eye Olho Ship Navio

Ribbon Fita Feeling Sentimento Occasionally Occasionalmente
Event Evento Sad Eua Visit Visita
First Primeiro Woke up Acordar Under Embaixo
Class Classe Quite Bastante False Falso
Certain Cert Once Uma Vez Pirate Pirata

End of lesson six test

Below you will find a short test which covers the sixth lesson. This short twenty minute test is meant as a revision and not as a marker for how well the student is progressing.

Tests all the way through these books are for motivational and revision purposes only. People perform differently under exam pressures and we believe that a student's primary aim is to learn a new skill and not to prove his or her worth. So, when giving the tests keep it light. The tests consist of ten yes or no questions and a short dictation containing some of the words introduced. You will also find the answering sheets below. Please feel free to print off as many as needed for each student.

End of section dictation.

Well, I have to say that they sold like hot cakes once we offered them for sale and were soon sold out. We had been throwing money at the product for over a year before they eventually became available. We had to take someone on to cope with the demand of the sales. The boy was found to have blue blood and soon joined the royal family. He certainly had been the blue eyed boy. We decided to take stock and make changes to our business. We had been throwing money at the marketing, and then out of the blue it all changed.

Ten questions about idioms.
Enter the missing words in the right hand column.

1 The products sold like _____ cakes.
2 We took _____ of the situation.
3 He threw ____ water on my idea.
4 He certainly was the ____ eyed boy.
5 When he arrived at work he was feeling a little ____.
6 The pirate ship was flying ______ colours.
7 He only visits his mother once in a ____ moon.
8 I told him to ____ while the _____ was hot.
9 I needed to see the contract in ____ and ____.
10 The business is about to ____ public.

Review the answers on the next page

Once the test is completed do a full review of all the errors and questions the student may have.

____

Test Answers

1	Hot
2	Stock
3	Cold
4	Blue
5	Blue
6	False
7	Blue
8	Strike, Iron
9	Black, White
10	Go

At this point in your studies do a full review of the previous sixty idioms before moving onto e-book three. The vocabulary content in this e-book will expand the student's ability to communicate greatly.

Lesson Seven

Each lesson in this section contains twenty English idioms with explanations. As with the other sections in this method the student repeats the idiom until the pronunciation is correct and the meaning is understood. Where possible the Portuguese equivalent is compared alongside. Each section contains sixty idioms and a short self-test at the end.

Animal Idioms (1)

121).

ANTS, PANTS, RESTLESS, EXCITED, WEEKENDS

Idiom	**To have ants in your pants.**
Meaning	**Means to be very restless or excited.**
Example	**The boys had ants in their pants. I told them to calm down.**

Question: Have you ever felt like you are so restless that you feel like you have ants in your pants?
Possible answer: Yes, I usually feel like that on the weekends.

122).

ASS, BEHAVING, COMLETE

Idiom	**To make an ass of yourself.**
Meaning	**To look stupid after behaving badly.**
Example	**Don't make an ass out of yourself. Think about what you are doing.**

Question: Have you ever made a complete fool of yourself?
Possible answer: Yes, I have and I felt like a complete ass afterwards.

123).

BAT, HELL, AROUND, CORNER

Idiom **Like a bat out of hell.**
Meaning **Means to be very, very fast.**
Example **He came around the corner like a bat out of hell.**

Question: Can you run fast?
Possible answer: No I never run anywhere, but my brother runs like a bat out of hell. He is very fast.

124).

SORE, BEAR, MEEDY, IRRITABLE

Idiom **Like a bear with a sore head.**
Meaning **Someone who is moody and irritable.**
Example **He got up this morning like a bear with a sore head.**

Question: After drinking alcohol, do you ever get up in the morning feeling like a bear with a sore head?
Possible answer: Yes, usually on Sunday mornings after a good night out.

125).

BONNET, BEE

Idiom **To have a bee in your bonnet.**
Meaning **To have something on your mind all the time.**
Example **She has a bee in her bonnet about something today.**

Question: Are you OK today?
Possible answer: No, I have a bee in my bonnet. I'm not happy.

126).

KILL, BIRDS, STONE, JOBS, SHOES

Idiom **Kill two birds with one stone.**
Meaning **To do two jobs together to save time.**
Example **I will go to the supermarket and get your shoes. That will kill two birds at one time.**

Question: What does kill two birds with one stone mean?
Possible answer: It means to do two jobs at once. To do another job whilst completing another.

127).

BITTEN, BUG, INTEREST, SUDDEN, BOUGHT

Idiom	**To be bitten by the bug.**
Meaning	**To develop an interest in something all of a sudden.**
Example	**I was bitten by the motorcycle bug and so bought a Harley Davidson.**

Question: Do you have an interest at the moment?
Possible answer: Yes, I have started riding a bike again. I was bitten by the bug again after I went camping and saw a lovely Honda and decided to buy one.

128).

SNUG, COMFORTABLE, WARM

Idiom	**Snug as a bug.**
Meaning	**To be comfortable and warm.**
Example	**I was as snug as a bug in my bed.**

Question: When in bed do you often feel as snug as a bug?
Possible answer: Yes, often in winter when the weather is cold.

129).

FLAG, BULL, BECAME, ANGRY

Idiom	**Like a red flag to a bull.**
Meaning	**Will make someone angry.**
Example	**It was like a red flag to a bull. He became very angry**

Question: What makes you angry?
Possible answer: Rude people on public transport makes me see red.

130).

HORNS, DECISIVELY

Idiom	**To take the bull by the horns.**
Meaning	**To act decisively and do it now.**
Example	**He took the bull by the horns and just did the job.**

Question: Is there anything you have been waiting to do?
Possible answer: Yes, I must take the bull by the horns and finish writing my book.

Word translations.

Bull Touro Bear Urso Yourself Voce mesmo
Flag Bandeira Sure Certo Have Ter
Horn Chifre Head Cabeça Ants Formiga
Snug Confortável Bee Abelha Pants Canças
Bug Inseto Bonnet Chapéu Winter Inverno
Bite Morder Bat Morcego Restless Inquieto
Kill Assassinar Hell Inverno Weekends Fin de semana
Birds Pássaro Make Fazer Usually Geralmente
Stone Pedra Ass Burro Mornings Manhã

Teaching Point

Practice the new words by repeating them over and over and ask the student to repeat the idiom by using the Tagging principle to prompt the student and then repeat together by using the Tandeming technique until the student can recite independently.

Animal Idioms (Cont.)

131).

CAT, RICH, BUSINESSMAN, YACHTS

Idiom **A fat cat.**
Meaning **Usually a rich and powerful person. A businessman.**
Example **Monaco was full of fat cats with yachts.**

Question: Are you a rich person? Do you know any fat cats?
Possible answer: No, I'm not a rich person. I'm quite poor.

132).

GRIN, CHESHIRE, WIDE, SMILE, PLEASED

Idiom **To have a grin like a Cheshire cat.**
Meaning **To have a very wide smile on your face.**
Example **He was very pleased with himself. He had a grin like a Cheshire cat.**

Question: Why are you laughing?
Possible answer: I just saw a friend of mine. She made me laugh, because she had a grin on her face like a Cheshire cat.

133).

BAG, SECRET, EVERYONE

Idiom **To let the cat out of the bag.**
Meaning **To tell a secret to someone.**
Example **He accidentally let the cat out of the bag. Now everyone knows.**

Question: If you were asked to keep a secret, could you avoid letting the cat out of the bag.
Possible answer: Yes, I'm good at keeping secrets.

134).

DRAGGED, DIRTY, UNTIDY

Idiom	**Look like something the cat dragged in.**
Meaning	**To look dirty and untidy.**
Example	**She looked like something the cat dragged in.**

Question: Do you always dress well?
Possible answer: No, for example I went out last Saturday and arrived home looking very untidy. My mother said I looked like something the cat dragged in.

135).

SCALDED, GHOST

Idiom	**Like a scalded cat.**
Meaning	**To go very quickly.**
Example	**He ran like a scalded cat after he saw the ghost.**

Question: Are you a brave person?
Possible answer: Yes, I think so. Although If I saw a UFO I would probably run away like a scalded cat.

136).

FIGHT

Idiom	**Fight like cats and dogs.**
Meaning	**Means to fight a lot.**
Example	**The children were fighting like cats and dogs.**

Question: Do you like your sisters?
Possible answer: Yes, but we fight like cats and dogs sometimes.

137).

Whiskers

Idiom	**Like the cat´s whiskers.**
Meaning	**To be better than the rest.**
Example	**With his new suit on he looked like the cat´s whiskers.**

Question: What do you think of my new motorcycle?
Possible answer: Its really nice. Like the cats whiskers.

138).

DINNER, DRESSED

Idiom **Like a dog´s dinner**
Meaning **Dressed very well or to be the best.**
Example **This is the dog´s dinner. I'm very happy with it.**

Question: When you got out with a woman on a date do you get dressed up?
Possible answer: Yes, last night I was dressed like a dogs dinner.

139).

MEANS, UNHAPPY, WOMAN

Idiom **A dog´s life.**
Meaning **Means to have a bad or unhappy life.**
Example **He had a dog´s life with that woman.**

Question: Do you know anyone who has a dog´s life at home?
Possible answer: Yes, my friend has a dog´s life with her husband.

140).

RAINING, HEAVILY, OUTSIDE

Idiom **Its raining dogs and cats.**
Meaning **To rain a lot. Raining very heavily.**
Example **Its raining cats and dogs outside today.**

Question: Is it raining outside today?
Possible answer: Yes, its raining cats and dogs.

Word translations.

Fat Gordura Secret Segredo DinnerJantar
Rich Rico Accident Acidente Dressed Vestido
Powerful Poderoso Known Conhecido Raining Chovendo
Businessman Empresráio Drag Arrasto Heavily Pesadamente
Yacht Iate Dirty Sujo
Grin Sorriso Untidy Desordenado
Smile Sorriso Fight Luta
Himself Se Whiskers Bigodes
Bag Bolsa Suit Terno

End of lesson seven (Forty minutes)

It's important at this point to review all of the words and idioms one more time before moving onto lesson number eight. Once the student is comfortable then it's safe to move forward.

End of lesson seven test

Below you will find a short test which covers the lesson above. This short twenty minute test is meant as a revision and not as a marker for how well the student is progressing.

Tests all the way through these books are for motivational and revision purposes only. People perform differently under exam pressures and we believe that a student's primary aim is to learn a new skill and not to prove his or her worth. So, when giving the tests keep it light. The tests consist of ten questions and a short dictation containing some of the words introduced.

You will also find the answering sheets and answer sheets below. Please feel free to print off as many as needed for each of your students.

End of lesson seven dictation

I decided to take the bull by the horns and stop having a bee in my bonnet about the problem. The young girl was acting like she had ants in her pants and could not keep still. I think it was because she didn't sleep very well last night. She told her mother that she was as snug as a bug in her bed. For some reason she got up this morning like a bear with a sore head. I suggested she went to bed early tonight.

Ten questions about idioms.
Enter the missing words in the right hand column.

---

1 To take the ________ by the horns.
2 Kill _____ birds with one ______.
3 Like a ______ out of hell.
4 He had ants in his ______.
5 Like a ______ with a sore head.
6 He was _______ by the bug.
7 He is a fat _____ in the business world.
8 She had a grin like a __________ cat.
9 He soon let the cat ____ ____ ____ bag
10 He got ready and looked like a ______ dinner.

Review the answers on the following page

Once the test is completed do a full review of all the errors and questions the student may have.

Test Answers

1	Bull
2	Two, Stone
3	Bat
4	Pants
5	Bear
6	Bitten
7	Cat
8	Cheshire
9	Out, of, the
10	Dog´s

Lesson Eight

Each section in this section contains twenty English idioms with student repeats the idiom until the pronunciation is correct and the meaning is understood. Where possible the Portuguese equivalent is compared alongside. Each section contains sixty idioms and a short self-test at the end.

Music Idioms (1)

141).

RINGS, BELL, SOUNDS, REMEMBER

Idiom That rings a bell
Meaning Something that sounds familiar.
Example Yes, that rings a bell, I remember now. Thanks.

Question: Can you remember a movie about a convict called Luke?
Possible answer: Yes, it rings a bell. Wasn't it Paul Newman?

142).

DRUM, HEAD, TEACHING, REPETITION

Idiom To drum into someone's head.
Meaning Teaching by repetition.
Example I had to really drum it into his head.

Question: Have you got a good memory or do you have drum things into your own head?
Possible answer: My memory is bad. People have to drum everything into my head.

143).

FIDDLE, FIT, HEALTH, CONDITION, RUNNER

Idiom	**As fit as a fiddle.**
Meaning	**In a very good condition of health.**
Example	**That runner is as fit as a fiddle.**

Question: Do you keep yourself healthy?
Possible answer: Yes, I go to the gym every day. I'm as fit as a fiddle at the moment.

144).

JAZZ, SOMETHING, BETTER

Idiom	**To jazz something up.**
Meaning	**To make something look better.**
Example	**I jazzed my car up before I sold it.**

Question: Do you have a car?
Possible answer: Yes, I bought an old car last week. I have been jazzing it up. It looks great now.

145).

MUSIC, COMPLIMENTS

Idiom	**It´s music to my ears.**
Meaning	**Some that makes you very happy.**
Example	**His compliments were music to my ears.**

Question: Were you pleased that Manchester United won the game last night?
Possible answer: Yes, I was music to my ears. I love Man. U

146).

STRIKE, RIGHT, NOTE, APPROPRIATE, STRUCK, MOTHER IN LAW

Idiom	**To strike the right note.**
Meaning	**To say the right thing at the right time. Something appropriate.**
Example	**He struck the right note with his new mother in law.**

Question: If I told you that you had won the lottery, would it be music to your ears?
Possible answer: Yes of course, I need the money.

147).

FALSE, INAPPROPRIATE, WRONG, STRUCK, CLOTHES

Idiom **To strike a false note.**
Meaning **To do something wrong or inappropriate.**
Example **He struck the wrong note with his family when he arrived at the party in his working clothes.**

Question: Did you get into trouble when you arrived home late last night?
Possible answer: Yes, but I hate striking the wrong note with my parents.

148).

TUNE, DECISIONS, IMPORTANT, BOSS

Idiom **To call the tune.**
Meaning **To make all the important decisions.**
Example **My boss calls the tune in decision making.**

Question: Who calls the tune in your house?
Possible answer: My mother of course. My dad thinks he does, but its my mother.

149).

SING, DIFFERENT, OPINION, SINSE

Idiom **To sing a different tune.**
Meaning **To change your opinion about something.**
Example **He is now singing a different tune since he lost his job.**

Question: Have you changed mind about buying that old car?
Possible answer: Yes, I decided to buy it after all.

150).

BLOW, WHISTLE, AUTHORITIES, BLOWER

Idiom **To blow the whistle.**
Meaning **To give information to authorities about something that is wrong.**
Example **Edward Snowden was a whistle blower.**

Question: Do you know who the whistle blower Edward Snowden is?
Possible answer: Yes, I read about him in the newspaper last week.

Word translations.

Strike Greve Opinion Opinião Really Realmente
Note Nota Since Desde Fit Informa
Appropriate Apropriado Blow Sopro Fiddle Violino
Law Lei Whistle Assobio Condition Condição
Party Festa Bell Campânula Health Saude
Arrive Chegar Ring Tocar Runner Corredor
Clothes Roupas Familiar Familia Jazz Jazz
Call Chamada Remember Lembrar Music Musica
Tune Sintonia Drum Martelar Ears Orelhas
Boss Chefe Repetition Repetição Compliments Cumprimentar

Teaching Point

Practice the new words by repeating them over and over and ask the student to repeat the idioms by using the Tagging principle to prompt the student and then repeat together by using the Tandeming technique until the student can recite independently.

Music Idioms (2)

151).

CHEAP, NOTHING

Idiom **Going for a song.**
Meaning **Being sold for next to nothing. Very cheap.**
Example **I will have to buy that car it´s going for a song.**

Question: Shall I buy that car or not? What do you think?
Possible answer: Yes, its going for a song. Very cheap.

152).

FINE, FINAL, TOUCHES, FINISHED, FIFTH

Idiom **To fine tune.**
Meaning **Means that putting the final touches to something.**
Example **I have nearly finished my fifth book. I just need to fine tune the grammar.**

Question: Have you finished your homework?
Possible answer: No, I'm just putting the final touches and fine tuning it. I´ll bring it in tomorrow.

153).

BLOW, TRUMPET, ACHIEVEMENTS, SICK

Idiom **To blow your own trumpet.**
Meaning **Means to boast about your own achievements.**
Example **I get sick of him blowing his own trumpet.**

Question: Are you very good at football?
Possible answer: Well, I don't want to blow my own trumpet, but I'm pretty good, yes.

154).

CLEAN, BATHROOM

Idiom **As clean as a whistle.**
Meaning **Means to be very, very clean.**
Example **My bathroom is as clean as a whistle now.**

Question: Is your house as clean as a whistle?
Possible answer: Yes, we have a cleaning lady in most days.

155).

DAB, PAINTING, NOWADAYS

Idiom **To be a dab hand at something.**
Meaning **Means to be very good at something.**
Example **I am a dab hand at painting nowadays.**

Question: Can you paint?
Possible answer: Yes, I'm a dab hand at painting.

156).

DAMPER, ENJOYABLE, INSTEAD

Idiom To put a damper on it.
Meaning **To make something less enjoyable than it should be.**
Example **Well, the rain put a damper on going to the beach today. Let´s go to the pub instead.**

Question: Did you want to go to the party tonight?
Possible answer: Yes I did, but my father put a damper on that. He wont let me go.

157).

DANCE, ELSE´S

Idiom **To dance to someone else's tune.**
Meaning **Means to do what someone else tells you to do.**
Example **I don´t like dancing to anyone else's tune.**

Question: Do you always do what your father tells you to do?
Possible answer: I don't usually like dancing to other peoples tune, but my dad is so strict.

158).

DARK

Idiom **Dancing in the dark.**
Meaning **Not really knowing what you are doing or where you are going.**
Example **I'm dancing in the dark with this, I need to get some help.**

Question: Do you know how to repair cars?
Possible answer: No, not at all. I'm just dancing in the dark with anything mechanical.

159).

DARKEN, DOORSTEP, RETURN, NEVER

Idiom **To darken someone's doorstep.**
Meaning **Means to never return to this place.**
Example **I told her to never darken our doorstep again.**

Question: If your father told you to never darken his doorstep again, what would it mean?
Possible answer: I would be very upset. Don't come back.

160).

TIRED

Idiom **Let´s call it a day.**
Meaning **To stop whatever you are doing.**
Example **I'm very tired now, let's call it a day and go home.**

Question: We have been working a lot today, shall we stop?
Possible answer: Yes, lets call it a day.

Word translations.

Song Cançoã Painting Pintura
Being Existir Damper Amortecedor
Cheap Barato Dark Escuro
Buy Comprar Darken Escurecer
Fine Fino Call Telefonar
Tune Adaptar Doorstep Porta
Final Final Whatever Por Mais Que
Touch Tocar Tired Cansado
Bathroom Banheiro
Nowadays Agora

End of lesson eight (Forty minutes)

It's important at this point to review all of the words and idioms one more time before moving onto lesson number nine. Once the student is comfortable then it's safe to move forward.

End of lesson eight test

Below you will find a short test which covers the lesson eight idioms. This short twenty minute test is meant as a revision and not as a marker for how well the student is progressing.

Tests all the way through these books are for motivational and revision purposes only. People perform differently under exam pressures and we believe that a student's primary aim is to learn a new skill and not to prove his or her worth. So, when giving the tests keep it light. The tests consist of ten questions and a short dictation containing some of the words introduced.
You will also find the answering sheets and answer sheets below. Please feel free to print off as many as needed for each student.

End of lesson eight dictation

My friend at work told me that he was going to blow the whistle on his manager today. He said that he had become a dab hand at taking things that did not belong to him. All of the stock at work was going for a song to employees so there seemed to be no reason to steal things. Anyway, he said that he was tired of dancing to someone else's tune. As soon as the clean-up is finished the better. Later that day the manager was told by the Managing Director to never darken his doorstep again. Now, we have a new manager calling the tune.

Ten questions about idioms.
Enter the missing words in the right hand column.

1 She said that rings a _____.
2 He is as fit as a _______ now that he has been exercising.
3 It´s _____ to my ears.
4 He is now singing to a ________ tune.
5 He is always _________ is own whistle.
6 The piano was ________ for a song, so I bought it.
7 You should never blow ____ own ______.
8 He is a dab _____ at painting nowadays.
9 Since he left, we have been ________ to the tune or another boss.
10 Her father told her to never ______ his ______ again.

Review the answers on the following page

Once the test is completed do a full review of all the errors and questions the student may have.

Test Answers

1	Bell
2	Fiddle
3	Music
4	Different
5	Blowing
6	Going
7	Your, Trumpet
8	Hand
9	Dancing
10	Darken, Doorst

Lesson Nine

Each section contains twenty English idioms with explanations. As with the other sections in this method the student repeats the idiom until the pronunciation is correct and the meaning is understood. Where possible the Portuguese equivalent is compared alongside. Each section contains sixty idioms and a short self-test at the end.

161).

SHAPE, UNHEALTHY, CONDITION, EXERCISE

Idiom **To be in bad shape**
Meaning **Means to be unhealthy and in bad condition.**
Example **My mother is in bad shape. I told her to exercise.**

Question: Are you fit or are you in bad shape?
Possible answer: I'm in very good shape, can't you see.

162).

ILLNESS, RECOVERY, NORMAL

Idiom **Back on your feet.**
Meaning **After illness. Your recovery. Return to normal.**
Example **After my illness I was pleased to be back on my feet**

Question: How are you feeling today? You were quite ill last week.
Possible answer: I was very ill, but I'm getting back on my feet now. Thank you for asking.

163).

BONES, SLIM, DIETING

Idiom **He is a bag of bones.**
Meaning **To be very, very thin or slim.**
Example **She is dieting too much. She looks like a bag of bones.**

Question: Has he been dieting again?
Possible answer: Yes, but I think he has lost too much weight. He looks like a bag of bones.

164).

KICK, BUCKET

Idiom **To kick the bucket.**
Meaning **To die.**
Example **My friend's uncle kicked the bucket this morning.**

Question: Did you know that the old man who lives down the street died yesterday?
Possible answer: Its really sad when someone kicks the bucket.

165).

BILL, HEALTH, DOCTOR, EXAMINATION, CLEAR, HEALTHY

Idiom **A clean bill of health.**
Meaning **After examination by your doctor, being given the all clear and to be told you are healthy.**
Example **After the medical he gave me a clean bill of health.**

Question: When you last saw your doctor did he give you a clean bill of health?
Possible answer: Yes, I am very healthy at the moment.

166).

BLIND, BAT, DRIVER

Idiom **As blind as a bat.**
Meaning **Can´t see anything.**
Example **The driver must have been as blind as a bat.**

Question: Is your eyesight good?
Possible answer: No, that's why I wear these glasses. I'm as blind as a bat.

167).

DEAD, DOORNAIL, ANIMAL, FOUND

Idiom **As dead as a doornail.**
Meaning **Really dead. Completely dead. No life left.**
Example **The animal we found on the side of the road was as dead as a doornail.**

Question: My radio has stopped working, can you repair it please?
Possible answer: I have already tried but its as dead as a doornail.

168).

DIE, BOOTS, DYING, GUY, DIED

Idiom **To die with your boots on.**
Meaning **Dying after living a healthy life.**
Example **Well, at least the old guy died with his boots on.**

Question: What's the best way to die?
Possible answer: What stupid question. So long as its with your boots on I don't care.

169).

DROP, FLIES, NUMBERS, FLU, EMPLOYEES, DROPPING

Idiom **To drop like flies.**
Meaning **To fall ill in large numbers.**
Example **The flu was making the employees drop like flies.**

Question: Have you been ill this year?
Possible answer: Yes, I had the flu last month. They were dropping like flies at work. Everyone had it.

170).

FROG, THROAT, POSSIBLY, INFECTION, SPEAK

Idiom To have a frog in your throat.
Meaning **To have a sore throat. Possibly an infection.**
Example **I can’t speak today. I have a frog in my throat.**

Question: When was the last time you felt like you had a frog in your throat?
Possible answer: Last month, I was quite ill.

Word translations.

Shape Forma Drive Dirigir Sore Ferida
Unhealthy Doente Driver Motorista Speak Falar
Exercise Exercicio Dead Morto
Feet Pés Nail Tacha
Foot Pé Door Porta
Bones Ossos Died Morreu
Kick Pontapé Boots Botas
Bucket Bomba Guy Rapaz
Bat Uma Throat Garganta
Blind Cego Frog Sapo

Teaching Point

Practice the new words by repeating them over and over and ask the student to repeat the idiom by using the Tagging principle to prompt the student and then repeat together by using the Tandeming technique until the student can recite independently.

Health Idioms (2)

171).

HUNG OVER, DRINKING

Idiom To be hung over.
Meaning To feel bad after a night out drinking too much alcohol.
Example This morning I had a terrible hangover.

Question: When was the last time you had a serious hangover?
Possible answer: A long time ago, I hate drinking too much.

172).

HANGOVER, BLOODY MARY, CURE

Idiom Hair of the dog.
Meaning To drink even more alcohol in the morning to cure a hangover.
Example I drank a Bloody Mary this morning to try and cure my hangover. But it didn't work.

Question: Did you have a hangover last Sunday morning?
Possible answer: Yes but I tried the advice you gave me and had a whisky for breakfast. Funny, I felt much better afterwards.

173).

SOUL, TOGETHER, SURVIVE, MANAGE, STRENGTH

Idiom **To keep body and soul together.**
Meaning **To manage to survive an ordeal.**
Example **After the terrible accident it took all my strength to keep body and soul together.**

Question: Is you life good at the moment.
Possible answer: Not really. Its taking me all my time to keep body and soul together.

174).

HEARING, LOUDLY, GRANNY, HEARING

Idiom **Hard of hearing.**
Meaning **Can´t hear very well.**
Example **You will need to speak loudly because granny is hard of hearing.**

Question: What is your hearing like?
Possible answer: I am a little hard of hearing, can you speak up please.

175).

CONDITION, SICK

Idiom **On one´s last legs.**
Meaning **In bad condition or about to die.**
Example **My car is on its last legs. I need a new one**

Question: The old man next door is very sick at the moment.
Possible answer: Yes I know, he is on his last legs.

176).

BORROWED, PERIOD, NEARLY

Idiom **Living on borrowed time.**
Meaning **The period of time after one has nearly died.**
Example **The old woman doesn't have much time to live. She is living on borrowed time.**

Question: The guy next door is very sick. Do you know him well?
Possible answer: Not really. But I heard he is on his last legs.

177).

MAKER, HUMOROUS, EXPRESSION, CAREFUL

Idiom **To meet your maker.**
Meaning **A humorous expression to describe going to heaven.**
Example **If you are not more careful in that car, you will end up meeting your maker.**

Question: Do you drive carefully?
Possible answer: I do now. I nearly met my maker last year so now I drive very carefully.

178).

LEASE, GREATER, ENJOYMENT, OPERATION

Idiom **A new lease of life.**
Meaning **A chance to live longer or have greater enjoyment.**
Example **She was given a new lease of life after the operation.**

Question: If I said my grandmother has had a new lease of life lately, what would I mean?
Possible answer: You might mean that she has found a new direction in life.

179).

KNIFE, HOSPITAL, DECIDED, PLASTIC, SURGERY

Idiom **To go under the knife.**
Meaning **To have an operation in hospital.**
Example **She decided to go under the knife and have plastic surgery.**

Question: Have you ever had an operation?
Possible answer: Yes, I went under the knife last year.

180).

GRAVE

Idiom **One foot in the grave.**
Meaning **Someone close to death.**
Example **He looked like he had one foot in the grave.**

Question: I'm feeling like I have one foot in the grave this week. What do I mean?
Possible answer: You are feeling older than you actually are this week.

End of lesson nine (Forty minutes)

Teaching Point

It's important at this point to review all of the words and idioms one more time before moving onto lesson four. Once the student is comfortable then it's safe to move forward.

Word translations.

Hung Suspender Bloody Sangrento Hearing Audição
Alcohol Álcool Soul Alma Loudly Alto
Terrible Terrível Together Companhia Grandmother Avó
Hair Cabelo Manage Gerir Condition Condição
Dog Cão Survive Sobre viver Borrow Emprestar
Cure Cura Ordeal Prova Dificil Period Período
Drank Bebeu Strength Força Nearly Quase

Maker Fabrican'te Lease Arrendamento Operation Operação
Humorous Engraçado Chance Oportunidade Knife Faca
Describe Descrever Enjoy Dresfrut Plastic Plástico
Heaven Paraiso Close Fechar Surgery Cirurgia

End of lesson nine test

Below you will find a short test which covers the ninth and final lesson of this section. This short twenty minute test is meant as a revision and not as a marker for how well the student is progressing.

Tests all the way through this book are for motivational and revision purposes only. People perform differently under exam pressures and we believe that a student's primary aim is to learn a new skill and not to prove his or her worth. So, when giving the tests keep it light. The tests consist of ten yes or no questions and a short dictation containing some of the words introduced.

You will also find the answering sheets below. Please feel free to print off as many as needed for each student.

End of section dictation.

You must be hard of hearing because you didn't hear what I said. Either that or you are still hung-over from last night. If you continue to drink like that every night you will end up meeting your maker sooner or later. If you want my advice, I would try and keep body and soul together at least until after the operation. When is it you go under the knife? After the operation, you will have a new lease of life. Just remember, the hair of the dog never worked for anyone. It just makes things worse.

Ten questions about idioms

Enter the missing words in the right hand column.

---

1 Are you ______ of hearing?
2 Last Saturday I was so _____-over I had to stay in bed.
3 After my holiday this summer I had a ____ lease of life and decorated my bedroom.
4 Next week I have to go under the _____ and have my operation.
5 I always drive slowly. I don't want to meet my ____ too early
6 It´s very important to try and keep body and ____ together after a funeral.
7 He is living dangerously and living on ______ time.
8 The old guy looks like he has one foot in the ____. Go and help him.
9 The hair of the _______ never cured anyone's hang-over.
10 The old guy died with his boots ___.

Review the answers on the following page

Once the test is completed do a full review of all the errors and questions the student may have.

Test Answers

1	Hard
2	Hung
3	New
4	Knife
5	Maker
6	Soul
7	Borrowed
8	Grave
9	Dog
10	On

At this point in your studies do a full review of the previous sixty idioms in each of the previous three books before moving onto e-book four The vocabulary content in these e-books will expand the student's ability to communicate greatly.

Lesson Ten

Weather Idioms (1)

181).

BOLT, HAPPENS, UNEXPECTEDLY, UNCLE, DIED, HEALTHY

Idiom	**A bolt from the blue.**
Meaning	**Something happens unexpectedly.**
Example	**The news of his death came as a bolt from the blue.**

Question: Have you ever received bad news like a bolt out from the blue?
Possible answer: Yes, my uncle died last year. He was healthy, so it came as bolt out of the blue.

182).

CLOUD, HAPPY

Idiom	**On cloud nine.**
Meaning	**To be very happy about something.**
Example	**I am so happy, I feel like I'm on cloud nine at the moment.**

Question: Are you happy at the moment?
Possible answer: Yes, I feel like I'm on cloud nine.

183).

HORIZON, PREDICTABLE, APPROACHING

Idiom **A dark cloud on the horizon.**
Meaning **A predictable problem approaching.**
Example **There are no clouds on the horizon at the moment. We are very happy.**

Question: Do you have any clouds on your horizon at the moment?
Possible answer: No, I don't think so. Everything is going to plan.

184).

GUESS, WEATHER, FAIR

Idiom **A fair weather friend.**
Meaning **To be only friends in good times.**
Example **He didn't support me. He is just a fair weather friend.**

Question: Do you have a lot of good friends or are some of them only fair weather friends?
Possible answer: Well, I hope they are all very good friends. But time will tell I guess.

185).

IMPORTANT, ARRANGEMENTS

Idiom **To be kept in the dark.**
Meaning **Not to be told about something important.**
Example **I was kept in the dark about all the arrangements.**

Question: Do you prefer to be kept in the dark about bad news?
Possible answer: Yes, sometimes. It depends on how bad the news is.

186).

HEAVENS, RAIN, LOODED

Idiom **The heavens opened.**
Meaning **Means in that it started to rain a lot.**
Example **Wow, the heavens just opened and now the roads are flooded.**

Question: Do you carry an umbrella with you in winter?
Possible answer: Yes, just in case the heavens open on my way to work in the mornings.

187).

ONCE, OCCASONALLY, BEACH, MOOD

Idiom **Once in a blue moon.**
Meaning **Just occasionally.**
Example **I go to the cinema once in a blue moon.**

Question: How often do you go to the beach?
Possible answer: Well, just once in a blue moon.

188).

REACH, AMBITIOUS, AVAILABLE, SETTLE, GUESS

Idiom **To reach for the moon.**
Meaning **To be ambitious.**
Example **If I was you I would simply reach for the moon and see where you end up.**

Question: After you left school did you reach for the moon or did you just settle for what was available at the time?
Possible answer: I went to college, then university and got a very good job. So, I guess I did.

189).

SHINE, REGARDLESS, DIFFICULTIES

Idiom **Come rain or shine.**
Meaning **Means to do something regardless of difficulties.**
Example **Lets go to the beach tomorrow come rain or shine.**

Question: How do you feel about going shopping this afternoon?
Possible answer: Yes, great idea. Lets go come rain or shine.

190).

POURS, EXPECTED, WORSE

Idiom **It never rains but it pours.**
Meaning **When things happen they are usually worse than expected.**
Example **Don't be sure. You know what they say. It never rains but pours.**

Question: Do you think bad news usually comes in three´s.
Possible answer: Yes, its true what they say. It never rains but it pours down with rain.

Word translations.

Bolt Lampejo Arrangements Organizar Difficulties Dificuldade
Blue Azul Flooded Inundada/o Shopping Compras
Cloud Nuvem Moon Lua Pour Servir
Moment Momento Occasionally Ocasionalmente Worse Pior
Horizon Horizonte Beach Praia Expected Esperado
Approach Confronto Ambitious Ambicioco
Predictable Previsivel Shine Brilho
Fair Justo Rain Chuva
Weather Clima Regardless Indiferentemente

Please note that translations are not literal. They are as close to the meaning of the idiom as is possible.

Teaching Point

Practice the new words by repeating them over and over and ask the student to repeat the idiom by using the Tagging principle to prompt the student and then repeat together by using the Tandeming technique until the student can recite independently.

Weather Idioms (2)

191).

RAIN CHECK, POSTPONE

Idiom **To take a rain check (US)**
Meaning **Means to postpone something.**
Example **Would you like to go to dinner this evening? Can we take a rain check? Maybe next week.**

Question: If I said, could we take a rain check. Would I mean?
Possible answer: You would mean that you need to postpone, but you would be happy to go at another date.

192).

CHASE, RAINBOWS, REAISTIC

Idiom **To chase rainbows.**
Meaning **To go after something they will never find.**
Example **He is always chasing rainbows. He needs to be more realistic.**

Question: Do you think it´s wrong to chase rainbows?
Possible answer: No, people need to aspire to greater things.

193).

STORM, BREWING, PRECAUTIONS

Idiom **A storm is brewing.**
Meaning **Something bad is about to happen.**
Example **I think a storm is brewing. We should take precautions.**

Question: When a storm is brewing, what do you generally do?
Possible answer: I usually take all the precautions I can to limit the impact.

194).

TEACUP, UNNECESSARY

Idiom **It´s a storm in a teacup.**
Meaning **Making unnecessary fuss about something that will soon pass.**
Example **His worries proved to be just a storm in a teacup.**

Question: Do you worry if you have arguments with your family?
Possible answer: No, because they are usually just a storm in a teacup and soon end.

195).

EYE, ARGUMENT, PROBLEM, SETTLE

Idiom **In the eye of the storm.**
Meaning **To be in the middle of a problem or argument.**
Example **I was caught up in the eye of the storm. It was really not my problem.**

Question: Have you ever been caught in the eye of the storm when trying to settle an argument?
Possible answer: Yes, usually with my younger sisters.

196).

WEATHER, ENDURE, SOLVED, CAUGHT

Idiom **To weather the storm.**
Meaning **Means to endure the problems until solved.**
Example **We simply had to weather the storm until the issue was solved.**

Question: When was the last time you were caught up in someone else's argument?
Possible answer: Just last week. My family were arguing were to go for our holidays and they didn't speak to each other for days. So I just weathered the storm until everything calmed down.

197).

THUNDER, SISTER, ARRIVED

Idiom **He had a face like thunder.**
Meaning **To look very angry.**
Example **My dad had a face like thunder when my sister arrived home at 3 am last night.**

Question: What do you do when your wife has a face like thunder?
Possible answer: I just go to the pub.

198).

TIDE, TREND, REVERSED, CHEAPER, EXPENSIVE

Idiom **The tide has turned.**
Meaning **When a trend has changed or even reversed.**
Example **I told you the tide would turn. Now things are much cheaper.**

Question: If you wanted to buy the latest iPhone, what would you do?
Possible answer: They are usually very expensive at the beginning but the tide usually turns after about six months and they become much cheaper.

199).

WEATHER, FEELING

Idiom Feeling under the weather.
Meaning **Not feeling well.**
Example **I was feeling under the weather this morning.**

Question: When was the last time you felt under the weather?
Possible answer: Last Sunday morning after I drank six caipirinhas

200).

STORMY, RELATIONSHIP, SIGN

Idiom **A stormy relationship.**
Meaning **To have a relationship full of problems and arguments.**
Example **No more stormy relationships for me. First sign and I'm out.**

Question: Are you still going out with Jim?
Possible answer: No, the relationship was a little stormy and so we finished the relationship.

Word translations.

Check Verificar Precaution Precaução Issue Um problema
Postpone Adiar Cup Xicara Solve Resolver
Dinner Jantar Pass Passar Thunder Trovão
Chase Perceguição Eye Olho Wife Esposa
Rainbow Arco-iris Argument Argumento Trend Direção
Never Nunca Caught Capturar Turned Volta
Realistic Realista Settle Resolver Reverse Reverter
Storm Tempestade Younger Mais Jovem Cheaper Mais Borato
Brewing Fermentar Sister Irmã Sign Sinal

Please note that some of the translations are not literal. They are as close to the meaning of the idiom or words as is possible.

End of lesson ten (Forty minutes)

It's important at this point to review all of the words and idioms one more time before moving onto lesson number eleven. Once the student is comfortable then it's safe to move forward.

End of lesson ten test

Below you will find a short test which covers the lesson above. This short twenty minute test is meant as a revision and not as a marker for how well the student is progressing.

You will also find the answering sheets and answer sheets below. Please feel free to print off as many as needed for each of your students.

End of lesson ten dictation

I have a lot of friends, but when a storm is brewing you find out who your real friends are. Whether they are fair weather friends or true friends will soon show, especially when there are dark clouds on the horizon. When faced with serious problems it´s usually best to face up to them and try and weather the storm. Come rain or shine the problems usually don't go away by themselves. We were walking home last night after work and the heavens opened. We both ended up looking like drown rats. Please don't spend your life chasing rainbows, get a proper job.

Ten questions about idioms.
Enter the missing words in the right hand column.

1 There are _____ clouds on the horizon this month.
2 He was just a ______ weather friend.
3 When I met him at the cinema he had a face like _______.
4 Its usually best to weather the _____ and wait for another opportunity.
5 It looks like storms are ______ . The business is in difficulty.
6 No one likes to be _____ in the ______.
7 Stop chasing _________ and find something productive to do with your life.

8 Come rain or _______ I will go go to the beach this weekend.
9 The heavens _______ and we all got very wet.
10 Who likes to be ______ in the dark about important issues?

Review the answers on the following page

Once the test is completed do a full review of all the errors and questions the student may have.

Test Answers

1	Clouds
2	Fair
3	Thunder
4	Storm
5	Brewing
6	Kept, Dark
7	Rainbows
8	Shine
9	Opened
10	Dark

Lesson Eleven

Each section contains twenty English idioms where student repeats the idiom until the pronunciation is correct and the meaning is understood. Where possible, the Portuguese equivalent is compared alongside. Each section contains sixty idioms and a short self-test at the end.

Relationship Idioms (1)

201).

FEATHER, TOGETHER, FLOCK

Idiom **Birds of a feather flock together.**
Meaning **Certain types of people stay or group together.**
Example **They are all crazy in that pub. They say that birds of a feather flock together.**

Question: If I was you I would stay away from that girl. All of her friends are really bad mannered.
Possible answer: Yes, I know My mother said the same thing and I think she is right, birds of a feather tend to flock together.

202).

INSIDE, MARRIED

Idiom **To know someone inside out.**
Meaning **To know someone very well.**
Example **They have been married for thirty years now. They know each other inside out.**

Question: Would you say you knew your boyfriend inside out?
Possible answer: Yes, I know him very well now.

203).

EXAMPLE, BOYFRIEND, GIRLFRIEND, COURSE

Idiom **To be an item.**
Meaning **To be a couple. Boyfriend and girlfriend for example.**
Example **Jack and Gill have been going out for six months now. They are definitely an item.**

Question: Would you consider yourself and your boyfriend to be an item now.
Possible answer: Yes, of course. We intend to marry.

204).

GOOSEBERRY, UNWANTED, EMBARRASSING

Idiom **To play gooseberry.**
Meaning **To be the third unwanted person on a date.**
Example **He guess her friend was just playing gooseberry for the night.**

Question: Have you ever played gooseberry on a friends first date?
Possible answer: No, never. It would be too embarrassing.

205).

HERDING, ORGANISE

Idiom **Like herding cats.**
Meaning **Trying to organise people that don't want to be organised.**
Example **Trying to organise this trip was like herding cats.**

Question: Have you ever tried to organise a lot of people to walk up a mountain?
Possible answer: Yes, once whist at university. It was just like herding cats.

206).

FLOW, EASIER, INCLINED, OBJECT, CONFRONTATION

Idiom **To go with the flow.**
Meaning **To go along with everything and or everyone.**
Example **Its easier to just go with the flow.**

Question: Are you more inclined to go with the flow or object to things.
Possible answer: I'm usually quite easy going. I hate confrontation.

207).

INVALUABLE, RAW, DEAL, TREATED, UNFAIRLY, BOUGHT

Idiom **To get a raw deal.**
Meaning **Thinking that you have been treated unfairly.**
Example **Well, when I bought my second-hand car, I now know that I got a raw deal and paid far too much money for it.**

Question: Do you think you are getting a raw deal with these English lessons or do you think you are learning a lot?
Possible answer: These lessons have been invaluable.

208).

SIGNIFICANT, USUALLY

Idiom **A significant other.**
Meaning **Someone important in your life. Usually your wife or girlfriend.**
Example **My significant other goes to university.**

Question: Do you have a significant other?
Possible answer: I used to have but she left me.

209).

RUB, SHOULDERS, FAMOUS

Idiom **To rub shoulders with someone.**
Meaning A brief encounter with someone famous.
Example **I love to rub shoulders with the rich and famous when I can.**

Question: Have you ever rubbed shoulders with anyone famous?
Possible answer: Oh yes, I once met Brad Pit at a party.

210).

CIRCLES, SOCIALISE, RICH

Idiom **To move in the same circles.**
Meaning **To be around and socialize with others.**
Example **I used to move in the same circles as Brad and Angelina.**

Question: Which circles to you move in these days?
Possible answer: I meet up with a lot of rich and famous people.

Word translations.

Bird Pássaro Girlfriend Namorada Flow Flui
Feather Pena Gooseberry Vela Everything Todo
Flock Bando Unwanted Nao desejado Everyone Todo o mundo
Certain Certo Third Terceiro Deal Acordo
Inside Dentro Date Data Treat Tratar
Married Casado Herding Tangendo Unfair Injusto
Item Item Cat Gato Wife Esposa
Boyfriend Namorado Trip Viagem Ruin Ruina
Shoulder Ombro Famous Famoso Ran Correu

Please note that some of the translations are not literal. They are as close to the meaning of the idiom or words as is possible.

Teaching Point

Practice the new words by repeating them over and over and ask the student to repeat the idioms by using the Tagging principle to prompt the student and then repeat together by using the Tandeming technique until the student can recite independently.

Relationship Idioms (2)

211).

THIEVES, THICK

Idiom **Thick as thieves**
Meaning **Very close relationship.**
Example **Bill and Ben were as thick as thieves at one time.**

Question: Do you have a very close friend Batman?
Possible answer: Yes, Robin and I have been as thick as thieves for years.

212).

APRON, STRINGS, ENOUGH, INDEPENDENT

Idiom **Tied to ones apron strings.**
Meaning **Still being looked after by mother when old enough to be independent.**
Example **Jason is still tied to him mum´s apron strings. It´s about time he left home.**

Question: Are you still close to your mother.
Possible answer: Yes, but I'm not tied to her apron strings.

213).

CROWD, COMPANY

Idiom **Two is company, three is a crowd.**
Meaning **Two people on a date is great. Three is too many.**
Example **I said to her best friend. Come on, two´s company but three is a crowd.**

Question: Have you ever been out on a date and taken a friend.
Possible answer: Oh no, two´s company on a date but three would be a crowd.

214).

LANGUAGE, BOSS, OBVIOUSY

Idiom **To speak the same language.**
Meaning **Means to agree on most things.**
Example **My boss and I obviously speak the same language. We get on very well.**

Question: Do you get on well with your uncle?
Possible answer: Yes, we have always spoken the same language.

215).

ORDERS, WALKERS, RELATIONSHIP, UNFAIR, UNFAITHFUL

Idiom **To give someone the walking orders.**
Meaning **The relationship has ended and the person is told to leave.**
Example **She was unfaithful and so I gave her, her walking orders.**

Question: Have you ever given anyone their walking orders?
Possible answer: Yes, my ex-boyfriend after he was unfaithful to me.
216).

MARCHING, LEAVE, ORDERS

Idiom **To be given your marching orders.**
Meaning **To be fired, to be told to leave.**
Example **She was given her marching orders after being late for work too many times.**

Question: Have you ever been given your marching orders?
Possible answer: No, never.

217).

STRANGE, BEDFELLOWS, UNLIKELY, PARTNERSHIP

Idiom **To be strange bedfellows.**
Meaning **Means an unlikely partnership.**
Example **My boss and his crazy girlfriend made very strange bedfellows.**

Question: What does strange bedfellows mean?
Possible answer: It means to be unlikely partners in something.

218).

STEADY. TWO-TIME

Idiom **To two time somebody.**
Meaning **To go out with a girl when you already have a steady partner.**
Example **She two timed me so she was given her marching orders**

Question: Have you ever two timed your partner.
Possible answer: No, I haven't. But if he two times me, he will be out on his ear.

219).

FIRMLY

Idiom **To be out on your ear.**
Meaning **Means to be told to leave very firmly.**
Example **I put him out on his ear after what he said to me.**

Question: Would you expect to be thrown out on your ear if you were rude to your father when you were a teenager?
Possible answer: Yes, he was very strict.

220).

LOGGERHEADS, DISAGREEMENT, DISAGREEING

Idiom At loggerheads.
Meaning To be in a serious disagreement with someone.
Example **My brother and I were at loggerheads for years.**

Question: If I said we were at loggerheads with each other what would I mean.
Possible answer: We would be disagreeing.

Word translations.

Thick Grosso Speak Fala Fellows Homem
Thief Ladrão Agree Concordar Steady Estavel
Tie Amarrar Obvious Obvio Partner Companheiro
Apron Avental Walker Andarilaho Ear Ouvido
String Corda Leave Deixar Firm Firma
Old Antigo Unfaithful Infiel Strict Estrito
Enough Suficiente Orders Ordens Rude Rude
Crowd Grupo Marching Marcha Disagreement Desacordo
Best Melhor Fired Despedido Brother Irmão
Company Companhia Bed Cama

Please note that some of the translations are not literal. They are as close to the meaning of the idiom or words as is possible.

End of lesson eleven (Forty minutes)

It's important at this point to review all of the words and idioms one in the last section more time before moving onto lesson number nine. Once the student is comfortable then it's safe to move forward.

End of lesson eleven test

Below you will find a short test which covers the lesson eleven idioms. This short twenty minute test is meant as a revision and not as a marker for how well the student is progressing.

Tests all the way through these books are for motivational and revision purposes only. People perform differently under exam pressures and we believe that a student's primary aim is to learn a new skill and not to prove his or her worth. So, when giving the tests keep it light.

The tests consist of ten questions and a short dictation containing some of the words introduced.

You will also find the answering sheets and answer sheets below. Please feel free to print off as many as needed for each student.

End of lesson eleven dictation

I recently finished with my girlfriend after I realised that she had been two-timing me. I thought we spoke the same language, but obviously not. As soon as I realised what was going on, I gave her, her marching orders. She was quite young and still tied to her mothers apron strings. So I guess this may have been one of the reasons why she left. My friend told me at the beginning of our relationship that we were strange bedfellows and that he wasn't surprised that she two timed me.

Ten questions about idioms.

Enter the missing words in the right hand column.

1 The two boys were as thick as _______.
2 The girl was still _____ to her _______ apron ____.
3 Two is _______ three is a crowd.
4 I thought we ______ the same language.
5 The woman gave her husband his _____ orders.
6 They were strange _______.
7 It´s wrong to two ______ someone.
8 If you continue to act like that you will be _____ on your ear.
9 The two brothers were at ______ over the issue.
10 Have you ever rubbed _______ with the rich and famous.

Review the answers on the following page

Once the test is completed do a full review of all the errors and questions the student may have.

Test Answers

1	Thieves
2	Tied, Strings, Mothers.
3	Company
4	Spoke
5	Marching
6	Bedfellows
7	Time
8	Out
9	Loggeheads
10	Shoulders

Lesson Twelve

Each section contains twenty English idioms with explanations. As with the other sections in this method the student repeats the idiom until the pronunciation is correct and the meaning is understood. Where possible the Portuguese equivalent is compared alongside. Each section contains sixty idioms and a short self-test at the end.

Relationship Idioms (1)

221).

BLANKET, RUINED

Idiom **Wet blanket**
Meaning **Someone who spoils other peoples fun.**
Example **He is such a wet blanket. He ruined our party.**

Question: If I said he was a wet blanket, what would I mean?
Possible answer: It means that he spoiled our fun.

222).

ARMCHAIR, CRITIC, CRITICISES, WORSE

Idiom **An armchair critic.**
Meaning **Someone who gives advice to something or criticises something without actually being involved.**
Example **I am sick of him being an armchair critic. He should actually try it himself.**

Question: Would you agree that there is nothing worse than an armchair critic?
Possible answer: Yes, I guess so.

223).

CANDE, BURN, FREQUENTLY, ESPECIALLY

Idiom **To burn the candle at both ends.**
Meaning **Means to be going to bed late at night whilst getting up very early.**
Example **It´s never easy burning the candle at both ends.**

Question: Do you often burn the candle at both ends?
Possible answer: Yes, frequently. Especially at the weekends.

224).

BASKET, CASE, COPE, DIVORCE, CLEARLY

Idiom **He is a basket case.**
Meaning **Someone who finds it difficult to cope with things in life.**
Example **After her divorce she was like a basket case.**

Question: Being a basket case means what?
Possible answer: It means that the person has gone through a difficult period in life and now finds it difficult to think clearly.

225).

COMPARISON, INTELLIGENT, SPORTS

Idiom **Can´t hold a candle to it.**
Meaning **No comparison between two people or things.**
Example **He is very intelligent but his brother can´t hold a candle to him.**

Question: Are you good at sports.
Possible answer: Yes, but I can't hold a candle to my brother, he is much better than I am.

226).

CARPET, TREATMENT, ARRIVED

Idiom **To give the red carpet treatment.**
Meaning **To be given or to give the best welcome or treatment.**
Example **The movie star was given the red carpet treatment when he arrived at the aeroport.**

Question: Have you ever received the red carpet treatment?
Possible answer: No, I'm not important enough.

227).

HOUSE, ORDER, AFFAIRS

Idiom **To put your house in order.**
Meaning **To organise your own affairs before criticising others.**
Example **I told him to put his own house in order before making such comments.**

Question: If I told you to put your house in order. What would I be really be saying to you?
Possible answer: You would be telling me to organise myself before criticising you.

228).

SUCCESSFUL, PERFORMANCE, WONDERFUL, BOUGHT

Idiom **To bring the house down.**
Meaning **To have a successful performance**
Example **The play was wonderful. The actors bought the house down.**

Question: Have you ever been to a play that was so good the performers bought the house down?
Possible answer: Yes I have. I went to see ¨River-dance¨ in Dublin whilst on holiday. It was wonderful.

229).

BARMAN

Idiom **To be given something on the house.**
Meaning **It´s free.**
Example **The barman said the last pint of beer was on the house.**

Question: Have you ever been given anything, on the house ?
Possible answer: Yes, last weekend after I sang in the pub. The barman gave me all my drinks, on the house.

230).

FLY, HANDLE, QUICKLY, MENTION, OWES

Idiom **To fly off the handle.**
Meaning **To get angry quickly.**
Example **He always flies off the handle when I mention the money he owes me.**

Question: Are you quick at flying off the handle?
Possible answer: No, I am a very calm person.

Word translations.

Wet Molhado Cope Lidar Wonderful Maravilhoso
Blanket Cobertor Divorce Divórcio Free Livre
Ruin Ruina Hold Manter Beer Cerveja
Armchair Cadeira Comparison Comparação Pint Caneca
Critic Critico Intelligent Inteligente Fly Voar
Actually Na Verdade Treatment Tratamento Handle Manipular
Burn Incendiar Order Ordem Angry Furioso
Candle Vela Criticise Criticar Quickly Rápido
Basket Cesta Bring Trazer Mention Mencionar
Case Caixa Performance Atuação Owe Dever

Please note that some of the translations are not literal. They are as close to the meaning of the idiom or words as is possible.

Teaching Point

Practice the new words by repeating them over and over and ask the student to repeat the idiom by using the Tagging principle to prompt the student and then repeat together by using the Tandeming technique until the student can recite independently.

Memory Idioms (1)

231).

BEAR, MIND, DECISION, DRIVING, PASSED

Idiom **To bear in mind.**
Meaning **To consider something when making a decision**
Example **Please bear in mind that I have only just passed my driving test.**

Question: If I said, please bear in mind that I am much older than you. What would I mean?
Possible answer: You would mean, I should consider your age.

232).

MEMORY, SIEVE, LOOSE

Idiom **Memory like a sieve.**
Meaning **To have a very bad memory. To forget things.**
Example **I always loose my keys. I have a memory like a sieve.**

Question: What did you say your name was?
Possible answer: You really do have a memory like a sieve.

233).

EAR, IMMEDIATELY, REALLY

Idiom **Go in one ear and out of the other.**
Meaning **To be told something and then immediately forget it.**
Example **I told him the time of the meeting but I think it went in one ear and out of the other.**

Question: What time did you say to meet tonight.
Possible answer: Oh really! I told you and it went in one ear and out of the other.

234).

SERVES

Idiom **If memory serves me right.**
Meaning **I remember it well.**
Example **If my memory**

Question: Do you have a good memory?
Possible answer: If memory serves me right, yes I think so.

235).

CONDITIONS

Idiom **On one´s last legs.**
Meaning **In bad condition or about to die.**
Example **My car is on its last legs. I need a new one**

Question: Do you have a car?
Possible answer: Yes, but it´s on it´s last legs I need a new one.

236).

CHATTED, TRIP

Idiom **A trip down memory lane.**
Meaning **Doing something or thinking about something from the past.**
Example **Seeing my old friend today was like taking a trip down memory lane.**

Question: When was the last time you took a trip down memory lane?
Possible answer: Last week. I met an old friend and we chatted over coffee for nearly two hours about the old days.

237).

REFRESH, FORGOTTEN,

Idiom **To refresh someone's memory**
Meaning **To remind someone of something they have forgotten**
Example **I could not remember his name until you refreshed my memory.**

Question: Can you refresh my memory please. Where did I leave my keys?
Possible answer: Yes, they are on your desk.

238).

FORGOTTEN, JOG, REMIND

Idiom **To jog someone's memory.**
Meaning **To remind someone of something that has been forgotten.**
Example **I had to jog his memory about the meeting today.**

Question: Can you jog my memory please? When is our next class?
Possible answer: Yes, it´s on Wednesday at 6pm.

239).

LOSE, TRAIN, THOUGHT, FORGETTING, ESPECIALLY

Idiom **To lose your train of thought.**
Meaning **To forget what you were just talking about.**
Example **I must be getting older, I keep losing my train of thought.**

Question: Do you think I'm getting older. I keep forgetting what I want to say.
Possible answer: No, its normal, everyone does it. I lose my train of thought sometimes, especially when I have a lot to think about.

240).

SENIOR, SUPPOSED, TWENTIES

Idiom **Having a senior moment.**
Meaning **Means to forget something like an old person sometimes does.**
Example **I just had a senior moment. Where was I supposed to be at 3pm?**

Question: Do you ever have senior moments?
Possible answer: No, I'm only in my early twenties.

End of lesson twelve (Forty minutes)

Word translations.

Bear Ter Serve Servir Jog Empurrar
Mind Mente Leg Perna Meeting Reunião
Consider Considerar Die Morrer Train Trem
Pass Passar Last Ultimo Thought Pensamento
Drive Dirigir Trip Viagem Lose Perder
Sieve Paneira Lane Rua Senior Senior
Keys Chaves Chat Conversar Old Velho

End of lesson twelve test

Below you will find a short test which covers the twelfth and final lesson of this book. This short twenty minute test is meant as a revision and not as a marker for how well the student is progressing.
Tests all the way through these books are for motivational and revision purposes only. People perform differently under exam pressures and we believe that a student's primary aim is to learn a new skill and not to prove his or her worth. So, when giving the tests keep it light. The tests consist of ten yes or no questions and a short dictation containing some of the words introduced.
You will also find the answering sheets below. Please feel free to print off as many as needed for each student.

End of section dictation.

You need to bear in mind that I have a memory like a sieve and that you will need to jog my memory once we arrive. The last time we met we sat and had a coffee for two hours whilst we took a very nice trip down memory lane chatting about old times. I tried to remember the name of the girl in the movie, but I couldn't, until you jogged my memory. I am always losing my train of thought these days. I must be getting older.

Ten questions about idioms.
Enter the missing words in the right hand column.

1 You have to bear in _____ that I am quite old.
2 I have a ______ like a sieve.
3 You told me last week but it went in one ____ .and _____ the other, sorry.
4 The old guy is on his last _____.
5 We took a ____ down memory _____.
6 You will need to _______ my memory once we get there.
7 To ____ one´s memory.
8 I am always losing my _____ of thought.
9 I just had a senior ________.
10 If my memory ______ me right its your round.

Review the answers

Once the test is completed do a full review of all the errors and questions the student may have.

Test answers

1	Mind
2	Memory
3	Ear, Out
4	Legs
5	Trip, Lane
6	Refresh
7	Jog
8	Train
9	Moment
10	Serves

At this point in your studies do a full review of the previous sixty idioms in each of the previous three sections before moving onto section four The vocabulary content in these sections will expand the student's ability to communicate greatly.

Lesson Thirteen

Age Idioms (1)

241).

GETTING, OLDER, EIGHTY, GRANDMOTHER

Idiom **Getting on in years**
Meaning **Getting older.**
Example **My grandfather is getting on in years now.**

Question: How old is your grandmother?
Possible answer: She is getting on a bit now. I think she's eighty years old in December.

242).

KNEE, GRASSHOPPER, RIDING, AREADY, CHILDREN

Idiom **Knee high to a grasshopper.**
Meaning **Only a small child.**
Example **When I was knee high to a grasshopper I was already riding a bike to school.**

Question: Do you have children?
Possible answer: Yes, but they are very young. My son is only five years old. He is only knee high to a grasshopper.

243).

SILVER, SURFER, FIFTY, ORIGINAL

Idiom **Silver surfer.**
Meaning **An older person using the internet.**
Example **I'm fifty eight years old now. Almost a silver surfer.**

Question: Do your grandparents use the internet?
Possible answer: Yes, they are the original silver surfers. They both use Twitter and have blogs.

244).

SPRING, GYM, ACTIVE, BECAUSE, NEITHER

Idiom **She is no spring chicken.**
Meaning **Someone who is a little old now.**
Example **My grandmother goes to the gym. But she's no spring chicken.**

Question: How active are your grandparents?
Possible answer: They aren't very active really because neither of them are spring chickens.

245).

HILL, ANOTHER, CONSIDERED, INDIVIDUAL

Idiom **Over the hill.**
Meaning **To old to do it now.**
Example **Another international marathon competition is out of the question now. He is over the hill.**

Question: How old would you have to be to be considered over the hill?
Possible answer: It depends on the individual. Some people age faster than others.

246).

TOOTH, GOING, PARTICULAR

Idiom **Long in the tooth.**
Meaning **To old to do something.**
Example **He is a bit long in the tooth to be going to discos.**

Question: What does ¨long in the tooth¨ mean?
Possible answer: It means to be too old to do a particular activity.

247).

MUTTON, LAMB, DRESSED, CLOTHES

Idiom **Mutton dressed as lamb.**
Meaning **Someone who dresses in clothes that are much too young for them.**
Example **Look at her! She is mutton dressed as lamb.**

Question: Does your mother in law dress in trendy clothes?
Possible answer: Yes of course, she always looks great. But she dresses her age. She certainly never looks like mutton dressed as lamb.

248).

ROB, CRADLE, MARRY, ROBBED, CERTAINLY

Idiom **To rob the cradle.**
Meaning **To marry someone who if far too young for you.**
Example **His new wife is far too young for him. He has robbed the cradle.**

Question: Would you marry someone much younger than yourself?
Possible answer: Maybe, but not too young. I certainly wouldn't rob the cradle.

249).

DIFFICULT, REALLY, THROUGH, GAINING, DIVORCE

Idiom **To put years on someone.**
Meaning **Something difficult in life that made the person look or feel older than they really are.**
Example **My divorce put years on me.**

Question: Have you ever gone through a crisis that made you feel much older than you are.
Possible answer: Yes, during my divorce. It was the worst period in my life. It felt like I was gaining years.

250).

OFFENDED, BEAUTY, RATHER, SLAP

Idiom **Age before beauty.**
Meaning **A rather rude way to say that someone should go before you.**
Example **You go through the door first. Age before beauty.**

Question: If someone opened a door for you and said, ¨age before beauty¨ how would you feel?
Possible answer: I would feel offended and probably slap him.

Word translations.

Grandfather Avó Grandmother Avó Trendy Doa ultima moda
Knee Joelho Gym Ginásio Rob Roubar
Grasshopper Gafanhoto Active Ativo CradleBerça
Ride Montar Hill Monte Divorce Divorcio
School Escola Consider Considerar Crisis Crise
Silver Prata Tooth Dente Gain Ganhar
Surfer Surfista Lamb Cordeiro Age Idade
Spring Primavera Mutton Carneiro Beauty Beleza
Chicken Frango Clothes Roupas Rude Rude

Please note that some of the translations are not literal. They are as close to the meaning of the idiom or word as is possible.

Teaching Point

Practice the new words by repeating them over and over and ask the student to repeat the idiom by using the Tagging principle to prompt the student and then repeat together by using the Tandeming technique until the student can recite independently.

Agreement Idioms (1)

251).

CLINCH, DEAL, FINALISE, FEES, AGREEMENT

Idiom **To clinch a deal.**
Meaning **To finalise something. Usually an agreement.**
Example **It took nearly six months to agree, but we finally clinched the deal.**

Question: Did you clinch a good deal with the fees for your English classes?
Possible answer: Yes, I got a very good deal.

252).

STRINGS, ATTACHED, HIDDEN, RESTRICTIONS

Idiom **No strings attached.**
Meaning **With no hidden restrictions.**
Example **I managed to get a bank loan with no strings attached.**

Question: Do you have a good school fees contract?
Possible answer: Yes I do, but there are strings attached. I must pay even if I miss a class.

253).

GENTLEMANS, SIGNED, WRITTEN, SHAKE, DELIVER

Idiom **A gentleman's agreement.**
Meaning **An agreement that is neither signed or written. Just on the shake of hands.**
Example **We have a gentleman's agreement to deliver the goods.**

Question: Would you ever make a gentleman's agreement?
Possible answer: It depends who the person is and whether I could trust him or not.

254).

SQUARE, DEAL, HONEST, ARRANGEMENTS

Idiom **A square deal.**
Meaning **An honest and fair deal.**
Example **An arrangement that is fair for both parties.**

Question: Do you always get a square deal at this school?
Possible answer: Yes, I have been studying here for two years and I have always been happy with the fees and the results.

255).

SEALED, COMPLETED

Idiom **Signed, sealed and delivered.**
Meaning **A completed deal or contract.**
Example **The deal to buy our new house is now signed, sealed and delivered.**

Question: Would you hand over the cash for a new car before the deal was signed, sealed and delivered?
Possible answer: No, not at all. I always make sure that I'm completely happy before I finalise anything.

256).

MATTER, FORM, CONTRACT, AUTOMATIC

Idiom **A matter of form.**
Meaning **To do something because it´s the usual thing to do.**
Example **I need to ask you to sign the contract as a matter of form.**

Question: As a matter of form, do you always lock the door at night?
Possible answer: Yes, I never forget. It´s almost automatic.

257).

LOCK, STOCK, BARREL

Idiom **Lock, stock and barrel.**
Meaning **All, everything.**
Example **He bought it all. Lock, stock and barrel.**

Question: If I said that I wanted it all, lock, stock and barrel. What would I mean?
Possible answer: You would mean all of it, everything.

258).

JUMP, GUN, EARLY, SOLD, CORRECT

Idiom **To jump the gun.**
Meaning **To do something, say something or think something too early.**
Example **He jumped the gun a little. The car had already been sold.**

Question: To jump the gun means to do something too fast. Is that correct?
Possible answer: Yes, it is.

259).

AGAIN, AGREE, LANGUAGE, DIFFICULT

Idiom **You can say that again.**
Meaning **Means that I agree completely.**
Example **Its very cold today! You can say that again.**
Question: Learning a second language can be difficult.
Possible answer: Yes it is, you can say that again.

260).

EXCESSIVE, BEAUTIFUL

Idiom **Over the top.**
Meaning **To be excessive.**
Example **Saying that to me was a little over the top.**

Question: If I said you had a beautiful body, would you hold it against me?
Possible answer: Yes, but that would be completely over the top.

Word translations.

Clinch Segurar Shake Agitar Form Forma
Deal Acordo Deliver Entregar Lock Gatilho
Finalise Finalizar Square Quadrado Stock Culatra
Agreement Acordo Both Os dois Barrel Canal
strings Complicaçãoes Parties Groupo Jump Saltar
Restrict Restrito Sign Signo Gun Arma
Loan Emprestimo Seal Selar Sold Vendido
Attach Anexar Contract Contrato Cold Frio
Neither Nem Matter Importar Top Topo

Please note that some of the translations are not literal. They are as close too the meaning of the idiom or word as is possible.

End of lesson thirteen (Forty minutes)

It's important at this point to review all of the words and idioms from the last three sections one more time before moving onto lesson number fourteen. Once the student is comfortable then it's safe to move forward.

End of lesson thirteen test

Below you will find a short test which covers the lesson above. This short twenty minute test is meant as a revision and not as a marker for how well the student is progressing.

Tests all the way through these books are for motivational and revision purposes only. People perform differently under exam pressures and we believe that a student's primary aim is to learn a new skill and not to prove his or her worth.

So, when giving the tests keep it light. The tests consist of ten simple questions and a short dictation containing some of the words introduced.

You will also find the answering sheets and answer sheets below. Please feel free to print off as many as needed for each of your students.

End of lesson thirteen dictation

I have known him since he was knee high to a grasshopper. He is always helping me with my Twitter page, because I keep forgetting my password. He says I'm a silver surfer, but I don't feel that old. I bought a a new computer system last week because I thought that maybe, it was my old equipment causing the problems. The salesman thought it would be a good idea to buy the whole lot, lock, stock and barrel. Then I would be up to date with everything I need. Although, I thought that might be a little over the top. Sometimes I think people think I'm over the hill but there is life in the old dog yet. Last night I met a beautiful woman but she turned out to be far too old for me. My friend said she was mutton dressed as lamb. So I made an excuse and escaped while I could.

Ten questions about idioms.
Enter the missing words in the right hand column.

1 I'm getting on in ______ now.
2 I told him not to jump the ______.
3 When she said I was a silver _____ I suddenly felt quite old.
4 Don't you think that 5,000 is a little _____ the top for a car of that age?
5 That woman was definitely ______ dressed as lamb and ugly too.
6 I have known that boy since he was ____ high to a ______.
7 I need you to sign this IOU as a matter of _____ please.
8 I promise you, there are no _____ attached.
9 I bought the lot at the auction, lock, ____ and _____.
10 Telling her she looks like mutton dressed as lamb was a little _____ the top. Don't you think so?

Review the answers on the following page

Once the test is completed do a full review of all the errors and questions the student may have.

Test Answers

1	Years
2	Gun
3	Surfer
4	Over
5	Mutton
6	Knee, Grasshopper
7	Form
8	Strings
9	Stock. Barrel
10	Over

Lesson Fourteen

Anger Idioms (1)

261).

INSULTING, ARMS, DEPENDS

Idiom **To be up in arms**
Meaning **To be angry or upset about something.**
Example **He got up in arms as soon as I said it.**

Question: If I said something insulting to you. Would you be up in arms about it.
Possible answer: Well, it depends what you say to me.

262).

ALIVE, CRITICISE, REALLY, DRESSING, CONVINCING, ATE, ARGUED

Idiom **Eat someone alive.**
Meaning **To severely criticise someone.**
Example **He really gave him a dressing down. He ate him alive during the argument.**

Question: Have you ever had such a strong convincing argument that you ate the other person alive?
Possible answer: Yes. The last time I argued with my younger brother. He tried to tell me that President Nixon was honest during Watergate.

263).

HOMEWORK

Idiom **To give a dressing down**
Meaning **To really tell someone off for doing something wrong.**
Example **He was given a right dressing down after what he did.**

Question: If I gave you a good dressing down for not doing your homework, what would you say?
Possible answer: I would that you were being a little over the top.

264).

COUNTER, DINNER, ARGUMENT, DEFEND, LAWYER

Idiom **To have someone for dinner.**
Meaning **Meaning that you really get the better of someone in an argument.**
Example **He tried to defend himself in court but the lawyer had him for dinner in his counter argument.**

Question: If I tried to tell you that learning English was very, very easy, what would you say.
Possible answer: Well, I think you would be wrong and I would have your argument for dinner.

265).

EXPENSIVE, IDEAL, FIREWORKS, MEANING

Idiom **Over the top.**
Meaning **Meaning to go too far with something.**
Example **The fireworks were a little over the top for such a small party.**

Question: Do you think that having English classes seven days a week is a little over the top?
Possible answer: Yes and expensive. I think three times a week is ideal.

266).

IMMEDIATELY, HABIT, FINGER NAILS,

Idiom **Cut it out.**
Meaning **Means stop it immediately or to stop a habit.**
Example **I keep trying to cut smoking out.**

Question: Do you bite your finger nails?
Possible answer: Yes I do. I know I should cut it out.

267).

DRIVE, IRRITATED, EVENTUALLY

Idiom **Drive someone up the wall.**
Meaning **To make someone crazy, irritated, annoyed.**
Example **That music is driving me up the wall.**
Question: If I kept asking you the same question over and over again. What would you say?
Possible answer: I would eventually say that you drive me up the wall.

268).

BEAR, SORE, TEMPERED, WOKEN UP

Idiom **A bear with a sore head.**
Meaning **Someone irritable and bad tempered.**
Example **He woke up like a bear with a sore head.**

Question: Have you ever woken up like a bear with a sore head?
Possible answer: Yes, every Sunday morning with a hangover.

269).

BITE, SRONGY, ANGRILY, APOLOGISE

Idiom **To bite someone's head off.**
Meaning Means to say something strongly or angrily to someone.
Example **OK, no need to bite my head off. I apologise.**

Question: If I said "OK, don't bite my head off" What would I mean?
Possible answer: You would mean that you didn't want me to speak in an angry voice to you.

270).

BLOW, FUSE, TEMPER, SUDDEN, PRETTY

Idiom **To blow a fuse.**
Meaning **To lose your temper all of a sudden.**
Example **He got so agitated that I thought he was going to blow a fuse.**

Question: Do you blow a fuse very often?
Possible answer: Not very often, I'm pretty cool about most things.

Word translations.

Arm Braço Counter Contrariar Blow Soprar
Alive Vivo Fireworks Fogos de Artificio Fuse Fusivel
Severe Grave Crazy Louco Suddenly De repente
Criticise Criticar Irritate Irritar Agitate Agitar
Dress Vestir Annoy Irritar
Ate Comi Sore Dolorido
Defend Defender Temper Temperamento
Court Tribulal Bite Morder
Lawyer Advogado Apologise Desculpar

Please note that some translations are not literal. They are as close to the meaning of the idiom and word as is possible.

Teaching Point

Practice the new words by repeating them over and over and ask the student to repeat the idioms by using the Tagging principle to prompt the student and then repeat together by using the Tandeming technique until the student can recite independently.

Anger Idioms (2)

271).

FLAK, BLAME, HAPPENED, YESTERDAY

Idiom	**To take the flak**
Meaning	**To take the blame for something.**
Example	**I took a lot of flak for what happened yesterday.**

Question: Have you ever taken the flak for something you hadn't done?
Possible answer: Yes, when I was at school I took the blame for something for my friend so she wouldn't get into trouble again.

272).

CRYING, EXPRESSION, FRUSTRATION, LOUD, FAILED

Idiom	**For crying out loud.**
Meaning	**An expression used to show frustration.**
Example	**For crying out loud. I told you to turn that music down.**

Question: If I said, ¨for crying out loud do your homework¨ what would I be saying to you?
Possible answer: You would be showing frustration because I failed to do my homework again.

273).

CHEESED OFF, ANNOYED

Idiom	**To be cheesed off**
Meaning	**To be annoyed and frustrated**
Example	**I'm feeling a little cheesed off today.**

Question: You look a little cheesed off today. Are you ok?
Possible answer: Yes, I'm fine. I just had a late night last night.

274).

BONE, PICK, DISCUSS

Idiom	**Have a bone to pick with someone.**
Meaning	**Means to have something serious to discuss with someone.**
Example	**I have a bone to pick with you about last night.**

Question: If I said, ¨I have a bone to pick with you about your homework¨what would I mean?
Possible answer: You would want to discuss it with me in a serious way.

275).

FLEA, ISSUE, KNEW, MOOD

Idiom **To have a flea in your ear.**
Meaning **Means to have an issue with someone about something.**
Example I knew he had a flea in his ear about something today.

Question: Do you have a flea in your ear about anything?
Possible answer: No, I'm in a very good mood today.

276).

PATIENT, FLY, LOSE, QUICKLY, HANDLE, TEMPER

Idiom **To fly off the handle.**
Meaning **To lose your temper very quickly.**
Example **He flew off the handle at me. I only said that I wanted to go home early.**

Question: Is there any need to fly off the handle with people?
Possible answer: No, people should be more patient with each other.

277)

FAIRY, FOAM, MOUTH, ANGER

Idiom **Foaming at the mouth.**
Meaning **To be extremely angry about something.**
Example **He was foaming at the mouth with anger. We had to sit him down and make him a cup of tea.**

Question: Have you ever been so angry as to foam at the mouth like an animal?
Possible answer: No, I am a fairly chilled kind of person about most things.

278).

BACK, FINDING, FAULTS, CONTINUALLY, USUALY

Idiom **Get off my back please.**
Meaning **Means to tell someone to stop finding faults with you.**
Example **Get off my back please before we start arguing**

Question: What do you say to people when they continually criticise you?
Possible answer: Usually, I tell them to get off my back.

279).

RUSE, GOAT, IRRITATES, PUBLIC, TRANSPORT

Idiom **To get someone's goat.**
Meaning **Something that really irritates you or someone.**
Example **That really gets my goat. I hate funk music.**

Question: What mostly gets your goat?
Possible answer: People being rude on public transport really gets my goat.

280).

TWIST, KNICKERS, UNDERSTAND, SOLVE, NERVOUS, FRUSTRATED

Idiom **Get your knickers in a twist.**
Meaning **To get nervous or angry or frustrated about something.**
Example **OK, don't get your knickers in a twist, we will solve your problem.**

Question: I would like you to have your homework in by Thursday, do you understand?
Possible answer: OK, I understand, but don't get your knickers in a twist.

Word translations.

Flak Culpa Pick Escolher Goat Cabra
Blame Culpa Discuss Discutir Knickers Cuecas
Happen Acontecer Flea Pulga Twist Torção
Cry Grito Ear Orelha Solve Resolver
Loud Alto Handle Punho
Frustration Frustração Temper Temperamento
Cheesed off Aborrecer Foam Espumar
Annoyed Aborrecer Mouth boca
Little Pouco Angry Irritado
Bone Osso Fault Falha

Please note that some of the translations are not literal. They are as close to the meaning of the idiom or actual word as is possible.

End of lesson fourteen (Forty minutes)

It's important at this point to review some of the words and idioms one more time before moving onto lesson number fifteen. Once the student is comfortable then it's safe to move forward.

End of lesson Fourteen test

Below you will find a short test which covers the fourteenth lesson idioms. This short twenty minute test is meant as a revision and not as a marker for how well the student is progressing. Tests all the way through these books are for motivational and revision purposes only. People perform differently under exam pressures and we believe that a student's primary aim is to learn a new skill and not to prove his or her worth.

So, when giving the tests keep it light.

The tests consist of ten questions and a short dictation containing some of the words introduced.

You will also find the answering sheets and answer sheets below. Please feel free to print off as many as needed for each student.

End of lesson fourteen dictation

For crying out loud, there is no need to fly off the handle with me just because you have a flea in your ear about it. I wish you would get off my back and let me sort the problem out myself. It really gets my goat when you do that. There really is no need to get so cheesed off over small things. In future, try not to get your knickers in a twist so quickly. If you have a bone to pick with me just knock on my door so that we can discuss any issues properly.

Ten questions about idioms.
Enter the missing words in the right hand column.

1 I'm not willing to take the _____ for you anymore.
2 For crying out ______ can you turn that music down please?
3 Yes I'm feeling a little ______ off about this now.
4 Listen, if you have a _____ to pick with me just say so.
5 This morning he had a ______ in his ear about something.
6 If you fly off the ______ like that again, I'm leaving you.
7 Please _____ off my back.
8 This is really getting my______. We need to solve the problem as soon as possible.
9 Don't get your ______ in a twist. It´s only work.
10 OK, don't blow a fuse.

Review the answers on the following page

Once the test is completed do a full review of all the errors and questions the student may have.

Test Answers

1	Flak
2	Loud
3	Cheesed Off
4	Bone
5	Flea
6	Handle
7	Get
8	Goat
9	Knickers
10	Fuse

Lesson Fifteen

Each section contains twenty English idioms with explanations. As with the other sections in this method the student repeats the idiom until the pronunciation is correct and the meaning is understood. Where possible the Portuguese equivalent is compared alongside. Each section contains sixty idioms and a short self-test at the end.

Anger Idioms (3)

281).

BONNET, DISCUSS, FRUSTRATED

Idiom **To have a bee in your bonnet.**
Meaning **To have an issue that you need to discuss.**
Example **What have you got a bee in your bonnet about?**

Question: If I said I had a bee in my bonnet about work. What would I mean?
Possible answer: You would mean that you were frustrated and needed to talk about something.

282).

CHEST, BOTHERING, MOMENT, CLASSES

Idiom **To get something off your chest.**
Meaning **Means to finally talk about an issue that is bothering you.**
Example **I need to get something off my chest. Can we sit down and talk for a moment?**

Question: Do you need to get anything off your chest?
Possible answer: Yes I do. Your classes are too expensive.

283).

HAIR, TACTFULLY

Idiom **To get in someone's hair**
Meaning **To annoy someone very much or they get in your way.**
Example **She was hanging around all day and getting in my hair.**

Question: If someone gets in you hair what do you do?
Possible answer: I usually try tactfully to tell them to go and find something to do.

284).

SKIN, ANNOYING

Idiom **To get under someone's skin.**
Meaning **Someone or something is annoying you.**
Example That person is starting to get under my skin.

Question: He is starting to get under my skin. What shall I do?
Possible answer: If I was you, I would just tell him.

285).

UNCOMFORTABLE, CRAWL, CREEPS

Idiom **It makes my skin crawl.**
Meaning **The person really gives you the creeps. Makes you feel very uncomfortable.**
Example **I hate that guy. He makes my skin crawl**

Question: Have you ever met anyone that made your skin crawl.
Possible answer: Yes, I met a guy a school. He really made me feel uncomfortable.

286).

SHALLOW, DEEP, FEELINGS, PERSONALITY

Idiom **Only skin deep.**
Meaning **Someone or something that is shallow in feelings or personality.**
Example **I get the feeling that his sincerity is only skin deep.**

Question: What does ¨only skin deep¨ mean?
Possible answer: It means shallow

287).

STARTING, PLAY, MIND, TIRED, WORKLOAD

Idiom **Its getting on top of me.**
Meaning **Something or someone is starting to play on your mind or making you tired.**
Example **The workload is starting to really get on top of me.**

Question: Does studying ever get on top of you?
Possible answer: It depends. If I am busy at work too, then yes.

288).

WORRY, SLEEP, PREVENT

Idiom **To play on your mind.**
Meaning **Starting to worry you.**
Example **That accident yesterday is playing on my mind. I can't sleep at night.**

Question: Do things play on you mind and prevent you from sleeping?
Possible answer: Yes, sometimes.

289).

NERVES, IRRTATE, WHILE, DRINKING

Idiom **To get on my nerves.**
Meaning **To annoy and irritate you.**
Example **He really gets on my nerves after a while.**

Question: Do you have any friends who get on your nerves?
Possible answer: Yes, Dave gets on my nerves after he has been drinking too much.

290).

Idiom **The hair of the dog.**
Meaning **To take more alcohol in the morning to cure the hangover you already have. More of the same.**
Example **Lets have a vodka for breakfast and try and cure this hangover.**

Question: When you have a hangover, do you ever take the hair of the dog the morning after?
Possible answer: No, that seems stupid. I usually just drink lots of water and that seems to work for me.

Word translations.

Bee Abelha Feelings Sentimentos
Issue Questão Play Jogar
Discuss Discutir Workload Carga de Trabalho
Chest Torax Sleep Dormir / Sono
Bother Incomodar Nerve Nervo
Hair Cabelo Dog Cão
Crawl Rastejamento Cure Cura
Deep Profundo Skin Pele
Shallow Raso

Please note that some of the translations are not literal. They are as close to the meaning of the idiom or the actual word as is possible.

Teaching Point

Practice the new words by repeating them over and over and ask the student to repeat the idiom by using the Tagging principle to prompt the student and then repeat together by using the Tandeming technique until the student can recite independently.

Annoyance Idioms (1)

291).

GLOVES, FIGHT, WHATEVER, ACHIEVE, WILLING

Idiom **The gloves are off.**
Meaning **Means that we are going to fight back now.**
Example **OK, the gloves are off. Whatever it takes to win now.**

Question: What would I mean if I said that the gloves are off now?
Possible answer: You would mean that you are willing to do anything to win or achieve.

292).

BALLISTIC, INDEED

Idiom **To go ballistic**
Meaning **To become very, very angry indeed.**
Example **He went ballistic with me when he found out the result.**

Question: Have ever gone ballistic over something?
Possible answer: Yes, when I found out my sister was wearing my new dress to the party.

293).

ANNOYING, RUBBISH, SHUT UP

Idiom **Give it a rest.**
Meaning **To stop talking about something annoying.**
Example **Oh give it a rest will you? That's total rubbish.**

Question: If I told you to give it a rest. What would I mean?
Possible answer: You would be telling me to shut up.

294).

PLAYING, HORRIBLE, CLOTHES, SCRUFFY

Idiom **To get your back up.**
Meaning **To make someone angry.**
Example **He really got my back up today playing that horrible music.**

Question: If I told you that your clothes were scruffy. Would it get your back up?
Possible answer: Yes, and I would probably give you what for.

295).

OFFICE

Idiom **To give what for.**
Meaning **To really tell someone what you think of them.**
Example **I really told him what for this afternoon when he arrived at the office late.**

Question: What does to tell what for mean?
Possible answer: To give someone a piece of your mind.

296).

PIECE, ARRIVED, TEENAGER, REBEL

Idiom **To give someone a piece of your mind.**
Meaning **To tell someone what you really think of them.**
Example **I gave her a piece of my mind when she arrived home at 4am.**

Question: Did your father ever give you a piece of his mind when you were a teenager?
Possible answer: Yes all the time. I was a rebel.

297).

UNCONVENTIONAL, YOUNGER, ROCKER, PUNK

Idiom **To be a rebel.**
Meaning **Someone who is unconventional**
Example **He was a bit of a rebel when he was younger.**
Question: When you were younger were you a bit of a rebel?
Possible answer: I was a punk rocker. So yes, very much so.

298).

DEEP, UPSET, REMEMBER

Idiom **Go off the deep end.**
Meaning **To go over the top when getting angry. Going too far.**
Example **He really went off the deep end this afternoon. I was very upset.**

Question: When was the last time you can remember going off the deep end?
Possible answer: I can't remember so must have been a long time ago.

299).

SPARE, REALISED

Idiom	**To go spare.**
Meaning	**To get very angry.**
Example	**He went spare this afternoon when he realised how much it was.**

Question: Did your mother ever go spare with you for arriving home late on a Saturday night.
Possible answer: Yes, all the time.

300).

HALF, SATISFIED, ACTUALLY, FINISHED, INSTEAD

Idiom	**My cup is half empty.**
Meaning	**Never satisfied.**
Example	**I'm only half way to fishing my books. No, I'm actually half finished.**

Question: What does ¨my cup is half empty¨mean?
Possible answer: It is a negative way of looking at something. Instead of seeing at as half empty we should think of it as full.

End of lesson fifteen (Forty minutes)

Teaching Point

It's important at this point to review some of the words and idioms one more time before moving onto section six. Once the student is comfortable then it's safe to move forward.

Word translations.

Gloves Luvas Upset Chateado
Ballistic Balistico Spare Sobressalente
Rubbish Refugo EmptyVavio
Late Tarde
Early Cedo
Rebel Rebelde
Unconventional Não convencional

Please note that some of the translations are not literal. They are as close to the meaning of the idiom or actual word as is possible.

End of lesson fifteen test

Below you will find a short test which covers the fifteenth and final lesson of this book. This short twenty minute test is meant as a revision and not as a marker for how well the student is progressing.

Tests all the way through these books are for motivational and revision purposes only. People perform differently under exam pressures and we believe that a student's primary aim is to learn a new skill and not to prove his or her worth. So, when giving the tests keep it light. The tests consist of ten yes or no questions and a short dictation containing some of the words introduced.

You will also find the answering sheets below. Please feel free to print off as many as needed for each student.

End of section dictation.

When he was much younger, Robbie was always fighting and getting into trouble. I guess he could have been described as a bit of a rebel who went off at the deep end at the slightest thing. He seemed to get peoples backs up and get into fights most days. He would arrive home with his clothes ruined and his father would give him what for. One day his father was so annoyed at him that he went completely over the top and off the deep end with him and promised that he would b confined to his bedroom for a week as a punishment. Of course Robbie wasn't happy with this and thought his father had gone over the top with the punishment and subsequently escaped through his bedroom window. But when Robbie arrived home again his father would give him a piece of his mind and double the punishment.

Ten questions about idioms.
Enter the missing words in the right hand column.

1 The gloves are _____.
2 His father _______ ballistic with him.
3 Give it a ______ please.
4 Hi seems to be able to get my _____ up very easily.
5 I gave him a ______ of my mind when he arrived home late on Saturday night.
6 He gave his son what _____ when he arrived home.
7 If he continues to behave like an idiot I will give him a piece of my ______.
8 Paul Newman was a bit of a _____ in some movies.
9 He always seems to go _____ at the _____ end.
10 Why is my cup always _____ empty instead of half full?

Review the answers

Once the test is completed do a full review of all the errors and questions the student may have.

Test answers

1	Off
2	Went
3	Rest
4	Back
5	Piece
6	For
7	Mind
8	Rebel
9	Off, Deep
10	Half

Lesson Sixteen

Beauty & Appearance Idioms (1)

301).

DRESSED, ATRACT, ATTENTION, KILL, COURSE

Idiom	**Dressed to kill.**
Meaning	**Dressed very well. So well, to attract attention.**
Example	**Wow, look at her. She is dressed to kill tonight.**

Question: Do you ever go out on Saturday night dressed to kill?
Possible answer: Yes of course. Every Saturday night. Is there any other way to dress?

302).

NINES, GLAMOROUS, CLOTHES, SMART, INTERVIEW

Idiom	**Dressed up to the nines.**
Meaning	**Dressed in very smart and glamorous clothes.**
Example	**Where are you going, dressed to the nines?**

Question: Where were you going yesterday? I saw you out, dressed to the nines.
Possible answer: I was going to an interview for a new job.

303).

BULLDOG, CHEWING, WASP,MISERABLE, UGLY, CHEER

Idiom **A face like a bulldog chewing a wasp.**
Meaning **An ugly person or miserable looking person.**
Example **What is wrong with you today? You look like a bulldog chewing a wasp.**

Question: Listen, you have to cheer up before we go out. You have a face like a bulldog chewing a wasp.
Possible answer: Oh, thanks very much.

304).

LOVE, MOTHER, HUMOROUS, OFFENDED, CRUISING, BRUISING

Idiom A face only a mother could love.
Meaning **A humorous way of saying someone is unattractive.**
Example **Your girlfriend has a face only her mother could love!**

Question: Would you be offended if I said you have a face only a mother could love?
Possible answer: Yes and if you did you would be cruising for a bruising!

305).

ACTING,RECEIVE,

Idiom **Cruising for a bruising.**
Meaning **Acting in a way that you are likely to receive a slap from someone.**
Example **If he says that once more he will be cruising for a bruising.**

Question: If you continue to say those kind of things to her don't you think you are cruising for a bruising?
Possible answer: Yes, I think so too. I will stop now before she hits me.

306).

VERTICALLY, CHALLENGED, SHORT, DOG-END

Idiom **Vertically challenged.**
Meaning **A short person.**
Example **How tall are you? About five foot and a dog-end.**

Question: He is vertically challenged isn't he? How tall is he?
Possible answer: He is only about 5 foot one inch I think.

307).

CIGARETTE, WOMAN,

Idiom	**Five foot and a dog end.**
Meaning	**Just over five foot tall. (A dog end is a cigarette end)**
Example	**That woman is short. She looks no more than five foot and a dog end.**

Question: How tall are you?
Possible answer: I'm five foot and a dog end.

308).

UGLY, GIRLFRIEND, SIN

Idiom	**She is as ugly as sin.**
Meaning	**Very unattractive.**
Example	**Your new girlfriend is as ugly as sin.**

Question: Have you seen my new girlfriend?
Possible answer: Yes, she is as ugly as sin.

309).

SPANNERS, PERSONALITY, UNATTRACTIVE

Idiom	**A face like a bag of spanners.**
Meaning	**An unattractive person.**
Example	**Good Lord. She has a face like a bag of spanners.**

Question: My new girlfriend isn't the best looking girl but she has a very nice personality.
Possible answer: You can say that again. She has a face like a bag of spanners.

310).

LOSING, MIRROR, NOTICED

Idiom	**Thin on top.**
Meaning	**To be losing hair on the top of your head.**
Example	**I just looked in the mirror and noticed that I'm going thin on the top.**

Question: If you were going thin on top what would you do?
Possible answer: I think I would have a Kojak.

Word translations.

Kill Assassinar Bruise Contusão
Attract Atrair Cruising Cruseiro
Glamorous Fascinante Slap Tapa / Bater
Smart Elegante / Inteligente Vertical Vertical
Bulldog Buldogue Challenge Desafio
Wasp Vespa Spanner Chave Inglesa
Miserable Miserável Bag Bolsa / Saco
Chew Mastigar Losing Perder
Mother Mãe Mirror Espelho

Please note that some of the translations are not literal. They are as close to the meaning of the idiom or word as is possible.

Teaching Point

Practice the new words by repeating them over and over and ask the student to repeat the idiom by using the Tagging principle to prompt the student and then repeat together by using the Tandeming technique until the student can recite independently.

Beauty & Appearance Idioms (2)

311).

SHAVED, MORNING,

Idiom **A Kojak**
Meaning **To have your head shaved.**
Example **I went to the barbers and asked for a Kojak this morning. What do you think?**

Question: Do you think my Kojak suits me?
Possible answer: You look like a slap-head.

312).

SLAP-HEAD, COMPLETELY, SHAVED, WEDDING

Idiom **A slap-head**
Meaning **Someone completely bald**
Example **You had your head shaved. Why?**

Question: Do you know anyone who is completely bald?

Possible answer: Yes, my husband is a slap-head.

313).

DECK, COMPLETE,

Idiom **To deck out.**
Meaning **To buy a complete set of new clothes.**
Example **We are going to a wedding on Saturday. I need to deck myself out with some new clothes.**

Question: When was the last time you decked yourself out with a new suit?
Possible answer: Just before my brothers wedding.

314).

CLOCK, UNATTRACTIVE, DARLING, ATTRACTIVE

Idiom **A face that would stop a clock.**
Meaning **Shockingly unattractive.**
Example **I can't even look at her. She has a face to stop Big Ben.**

Question: Do you think I'm attractive darling?
Possible answer: In truth, I think you have face that would stop any clock.

315).

SIGHT, TERRIBLE, IMPECCABLE

Idiom **To look a sight.**
Meaning **Someone who is dressed and looks terrible.**
Example **Did you see Marjorie at the wedding. Didn't she look a sight?**

Question: Do you ever go out looking a sight?
Possible answer: No, I always look impeccable when I go out.

316).

SHADOW, EVENING, SHAVE

Idiom **A five o'clock shadow.**
Meaning **Someone due for a shave. Usually in the evening**
Example **I need a shave before we go for dinner. I have a five o'clock shadow.**

Question: Do you usually get a five o'clock shadow?
Possible answer: No, not usually, I am a woman after all.

317).

UGLY, DUCKLING, MIGHT, APPEAR, TAUGHT

Idiom **An ugly duckling.**
Meaning **Someone who might appear a little plain looking.**
Example **She is the ugly duckling of the family.**

Question: Do you know the old song. There once was an ugly duckling?
Possible answer: Yes, I was taught it when I was a child.

318).

MILLION, FANTASTIC, PLEASED

Idiom **Looks like a million dollars**
Meaning **Looks fantastic.**
Example **You look like a million dollars this evening darling.**

Question: If I said, you look a million dollars would you be pleased?
Possible answer: Yes of course. But I would be wondering why.

319).

FROG, ATTRACTIVE, NICE, GIRLFRIEND

Idiom **Frog-face.**
Meaning **Not attractive all.**
Example **She is a frog face.**

Question: My ex-girlfriend had a lovely personality but she was a bit of a frog-face.
Possible answer: That's not nice. I'm sure she was lovely.

320).

BEAUTY, SKIN, DEEP, PERSONALITY, REAL, GENERALLY

Idiom **Beauty is only skin deep.**
Meaning **Beauty can be only what you see on the surface. The real beauty is below the skin, in someone's personality.**
Example **She wasn't a nice person. You know what they say. Beauty is only skin deep.**

Question: Do you generally go for someone with a good personality or someone who is pretty, or both?
Possible answer: I prefer a good personality. Beauty is only skin deep.

Word translations.

Shave Barbear Plain Simples
Barber Barbeiro Darling Amado / Querido
Bald Careca Frog Sapo Slap-head Careca
Wedding Casamento Clock Relogio
Ugly Feio Duckling Patinho Appear Aparecer

Please note that some of the translations are not literal. They are as close too the meaning of the idiom or word as is possible.

End of lesson sixteen (Forty minutes)

End of lesson sixteen test

Below you will find a short test which covers the lesson above. This short twenty minute test is meant as a revision and not as a marker for how well the student is progressing.
Tests all the way through these books are for motivational and revision purposes only. People perform differently under exam pressures and we believe that a student's primary aim is to learn a new skill and not to prove his or her worth. So, when giving the tests keep it light. The tests consist of ten simple questions and a short dictation containing some of the words introduced. You will also find the answering sheets and answer sheets below. Please feel free to print off as many as needed for each of your students.

End of lesson sixteen dictation

Before I meet my date tonight I have decided to have a change of hairstyle, so I will be going to the barbers to have my head shaved like Kojak. The last girl I dated loved it, but she had a face like a bag of spanners so the relationship didn't last too long. I don't mind if they are a bit of a frog-face but I do like a good personality. My sister has a very nice friend and I'm hoping to take her out one day. But I'm not sure she isn't interested in a guy who only sees beauty skin deep. You could say I'm quite shallow. Although, I'm not sure there is anything wrong with avoiding women with faces that could stop a clock. After my haircut I'm going to buy a new suit to impress my new girlfriend. I think its important to look like a million dollars on the first date.

Ten questions about idioms.
Enter the missing words in the right hand column.

1 He is a _____ head.
2 I need to deck myself _____ with a new suit on Saturday.
3 She has a _____ that could stop a _____.
4 She looked a _____ this morning when she arrived for work.
5 A always get a _____ o'clock _____.
6 My sister was the ugly _______ in the family. But she grew into a beautiful swan.
7 My wife always looks a ______ dollars.
8 She is a bit of a _____ face.
9 Beauty is _____ skin deep.
10 He had a face like a bag of _______.

Review the answers on the following page

Once the test is completed do a full review of all the errors and questions the student may have.

Test Answers

1	Slap
2	Out
3	Face, Clock
4	Sight
5	Five, Shadow
6	Duckling
7	Million
8	Frog
9	Skin
10	Spanners

Lesson Seventeen

Each contains twenty English idioms with meaning and examples. The student repeats the idiom until the pronunciation is correct and the meaning is understood. Where possible the Portuguese equivalent is compared alongside. Each section contains sixty idioms and a short self-test at the end.

Fear & Anxiety Idioms (1)

321).

BLOOD, BOIL

Idiom **To make your blood boil.**
Meaning **To make you angry.**
Example **That woman makes my blood boil.**

Question: Is there anyone in your life at the moment that regularly makes your blood boil?
Possible answer: Yes, there is a woman at work. She is so annoying.

322).

IGNORANCE, WORRY, BLISS

Idiom **Ignorance is bliss.**
Meaning **If I don't know about a problem I wont worry about it.**
Example **I prefer not to know. Ignorance is bliss.**

Question: What does the idiom, ¨ignorance is bliss¨ mean?
Possible answer: It mean that, sometimes its better not to know.

323).

FELT, FRIGHTENING, ANXIOUS, SCARED, UNFOLD

Idiom **My heart was in my mouth.**
Meaning **Someone who is extremely anxious about something.**
Example **I was so scared. For a moment my heart was in my mouth.**

Question: As she watched the terrible accident unfold, she had her heart in her mouth. How did you feel watching it?
Possible answer: I felt the same way. It was so frightening.

324).

BREATH, THOUSANDS, EMPLOYEES

Idiom **Don't hold your breath.**
Meaning **Waiting for something to happen and feeling anxious about it.**
Example **I hope we win the lottery one day. Don't hold your breath. It will never happen.**

Question: How do you feel about winning that new car in the competition at work?
Possible answer: There are thousands of employees with tickets so don't hold your breath.

325).

BOUGHT, CAMERA, RUBBISH, BURNT, UNSUCCESSFUL

Idiom **Don't get your fingers burnt.**
Meaning **Meaning someone suffering as a result of something unsuccessful.**
Example **I bought a car off the internet which turned out to be a wreck. I wont get my fingers burnt like that again.**

Question: Have you ever got your fingers burnt and lost a lot of money?
Possible answer: Not a lot of money but I bought a camera off Ebay once and it was rubbish.

326).

BUNDLE, NERVES, WAITING, INTERVIEWS, USUALLY

Idiom **A bundle of nerves.**
Meaning **To be very nervous.**
Example **She was a bundle of nerves waiting for her interview.**

Question: How do you feel at interviews?
Possible answer: I'm usually a bundle of nerves.

327).

NATURAL, BUTTERFLIES, STOMACH, NERVOUS

Idiom **To have butterflies in your stomach.**
Meaning **To have a nervous feeling in your stomach.**
Example **Waiting for the train, I had butterflies in my stomach.**

Question: Do you get butterflies in your stomach waiting for interviews?
Possible answer: Yes, all the time. Its natural.

328).

REACTION, BREAK, SWEAT, NERVOUSNESS, FEELING

Idiom **Break into a cold sweat.**
Meaning **A feeling of nervousness. Sweating a lot but feeling cold at the same time. So nervous that you feel sick.**
Example **I broke into a cold sweat as I waited for the answer.**

Question: Have you ever broke into a cold sweat because you were so nervous?
Possible answer: Yes, many times. Its a normal reaction.

329).

AFFRAID, BROTHER, SHADOW, ESPECIALLY, CAMPING

Idiom **Afraid of ones own shadow.**
Meaning **To be afraid of almost everything.**
Example **He was afraid of his own shadow whilst we were camping last weekend.**

Question: Are you usually brave?
Possible answer: Yes, but my brother can be afraid of his own shadow. Especially in the dark.

330).

EXCITED, CAT, BRICKS, RESTLESS, ARRIVE

Idiom **Like a cat on hot bricks.**
Meaning **Very nervous or restless. can't sit still.**
Example **He was like a cat on hot bricks waiting for Christmas morning to arrive.**

Question: Do you get excited at Christmas?
Possible answer: Yes, every year. I'm like a cat on hot bricks.

Word translations.

Blood Sangue Win Ganhar Answer Resposta
Boil Ferver / Cozinhar Fingers Dedos Afraid Com Medo
Ignorance Ignorância Burnt Queimado Shadow Sombra
Bliss Feliz Butterflies Borboleta Camping Camping
Heart Coração Stomach Estomago Cat Gato
Anxious Ansioso Sweat Suor Brick Tijolo
Scared Assustado Break Quebrar Christmas Natal
Breath Resiração Sick Doente
Feeling Sentimento Cold Frio

Please note that some translations are not literal. They are as close to the meaning of the idiom and word as is possible.

Teaching Point

Practice the new words by repeating them over and over and ask the student to repeat the idioms by using the Tagging principle to prompt the student and then repeat together by using the Tandeming technique until the student can recite independently.

Anxiety & Fear Idioms (2)

331).

BAITED, BREATH, IMMINENT, EXCITED

Idiom **To wait with baited breath**
Meaning **Excited about something that is imminent.**
Example **We waited with baited breath for the postman to arrive.**

Question: If you knew you had won the lottery, would you be waiting with baited breath to find out how much you had won.
Possible answer: Of course I would. I would have spent half of it by now.

332).

RUN, SCARES, ACCIDENT, SCHOOL

Idiom **To make ones blood run cold.**
Meaning **Something that scares you a lot.**
Example **When I saw the accident it made my blood run cold.**

Question: If I told you there had been a serious accident outside the school. How would you feel?
Possible answer: It would make my blood run cold until I knew everyone was ok.

333).

CHEQUE, WINNING, EDGE, WHISTLE, FINAL, HAPPEN

Idiom **To be on the edge of your seat.**
Meaning **Means to be anxiously waiting for something to happen.**
Example **I was on the edge of my seat waiting for the final whistle to go and my soccer team had won the cup.**

Question: Would you be on the edge of your seat waiting for your lottery winning cheque to arrive?
Possible answer: Yes of course.

334).

STRESSED, STAND, PRESSURE, INVOLVED, STARTED, PROJECT, PACE

Idiom **I can't stand the pace.**
Meaning **I can't stand the pressure involved.**
Example **If you can't stand the pace, you should not have started this project.**

Question: How do you feel when the pace of life gets too much for you?
Possible answer: It makes me feel very stressed.

335).

HEAT, PREVIOUS, SIMILAR, KITCHEN

Idiom **Can't stand the heat.**
Meaning **Similar to the previous idiom.**
Example **The pace of this is too fast for me.**

Question: What would I mean if I said if you can't stand the heat, get out of the kitchen?
Possible answer: You would mean that something is too difficult for me so stop doing it and I should let someone else do it.

336).

HEART, MISSED, BEAT, NEARLY, SCORED, WINNING, EQUALISED

Idiom **My heart missed a beat.**
Meaning **A sudden feeling of excitement. The feeling you get.**
Example **My heart missed a beat when Chelsea nearly scored the winning goal.**

Question: Did you watch the Manchester United v Chelsea match on Sunday?
Possible answer: Yes, my heart missed a beat when Chelsea almost equalised with a minute to the end of the match.

337)

WITS, WORRIED, PATIENCE, LOSING

Idiom **At my wits end.**
Meaning **Worried, losing patience with something.**
Example **I was at my wits end waiting for my daughter to arrive home on Saturday night.**

Question: Did your parents worry about you when you were a teenager?
Possible answer: Oh yes, my mum was nearly always at her wits end with me. She used to stay up until she knew I was safe.

338).

TONGUE, TIED, PROPERLY, INTERVIEWS

Idiom **Tongue tied.**
Meaning **can't speak properly when you are nervous.**
Example **When I get over-excited I usually get tongue tied.**

Question: Do you get tongue tied in job interviews?
Possible answer: Yes, all the time.

339).

SHAKE, LEAF, TERRIBLE

Idiom **To shake like a leaf.**
Meaning **So nervous that you can't stop shaking.**
Example **I was shaking like a leaf until I knew she was ok.**

Question: Do you shake very much when you get nervous?
Possible answer: Yes, sometimes its terrible.

340).

PINS, NEEDLES

Idiom **To be on pins and needles.**
Meaning **Worried about what's about to happen.**
Example **She was on pins and needles, she just could not stand still.**

Question: I was on pins and needles until I received the confirmation of my new job.
Possible answer: Were you? You don't seem the nervous type.

Word translations.

Bait Isca Pressure Pressão Score Contagem
Breath Resiração Involve Envolver Goal Gol
Imminent Iminente Project Projeto Patience Paciência
Postman Carteiro Heat Calor Daughter Filha
Run Corrida Kitchen Cozinha Tongue Lingua
Scare Susto Fast Rapido Tie Amarrar
Edge Borda I Idiom Idioma Leaf Folha
Seat Cadeira Miss Perder Shake Agitar / Tremer
Team Equipe Beat Bater Pin Pino
Pace Passo Sudden Repentino Needle Agulha

Please note that some of the translations are not literal. They are as close to the meaning of the idiom or actual word as is possible.

End of lesson Seventeen (Forty minutes)

End of lesson test

Below you will find a short test which covers the seventeenth lesson idioms. This short twenty minute test is meant as a revision and not as a marker for how well the student is progressing.

Tests all the way through these books are for motivational and revision purposes only. People perform differently under exam pressures and we believe that a student's primary aim is to learn a new skill and not to prove his or her worth.

So, when giving the tests keep it light.

The tests consist of ten questions and a short dictation containing some of the words introduced.

You will also find the answering sheets and answer sheets below. Please feel free to print off as many as needed for each student.

End of lesson seventeen dictation

I waited with baited breath for the match to begin because we needed to win this game. As the match progressed I found myself sitting on the edge on my seat. In the twentieth minute Manchester United almost scored a goal and my heart missed a beat. At half time they took Rooney off because he was unable to stand the pace of the game. The rest of the team were at their wits end with Rooney because he wasn't playing well. I had to stand up and fetch a cup of tea because I had pins and needles in my legs. As the game finished with a 2 -0 score line, I was tongue tied as to why Stoke City had played so badly.

Ten questions about idioms.
Enter the missing words in the right hand column.

1 I waited with baited _______.
2 I was at my ______ end with him.
3 As the care flew by at speed my heart missed a _______.
4 If you can't stand the _____, get out of the kitchen.
5 That movie made my ______ run cold.
6 I was on the ______ of my seat.
7 I had ______ and ______ in my legs.
8 After the horror movie finished I was _____ like a leaf.
9 The marathon runner could not _____ the pace and dropped out at twenty miles.
10 She could not think of what to say. I have never know her to be ____ tied before.

Review the answers on the following page

Once the test is completed do a full review of all the errors and questions the student may have.

It's important to note that each book carries the same introduction and instruction as the first book. This is so that any stage of instruction can be bought if your student has a higher level of English than a complete beginner. You can buy a stage four book and still learn about the method of teaching without buying the whole series.

Test Answers

1	Breath
2	Wits
3	Beat
4	Heat
5	Blood
6	Edge
7	Pins, Needles
8	Shaking
9	Stand
10	Tongue

Lesson Eighteen

Each section contains twenty English idioms with explanations. As with the other sections in this method the student repeats the idiom until the pronunciation is correct and the meaning is understood. Where possible the Portuguese equivalent is compared alongside. Each section contains sixty idioms and a short self-test at the end.

Music & Sound Idioms (2)

341).

RING, BELL, SOUNDING, FAMILIAR

Idiom **Ring a bell**
Meaning **Something sounding familiar.**
Example **His name rings a bell.**

Question: Does his name ring a bell to you?
Possible answer: Yes it does, but I can't remember where I know him from.

342).

FIDDLE, HEALTHY, FIT, GYM

Idiom **As fit as a fiddle.**
Meaning **Someone who is very fit and healthy.**
Example **She has been going to the gym for nearly a year. She is as fit as a fiddle.**

Question: Do you go to the gym?
Possible answer: Yes, I'm as fit as a fiddle.

343).

BURNED, REMAIN,UNDONE. HAIRDRESSERS

Idiom **Fiddling while Rome burned.**
Meaning **Someone doing something unimportant while the important things remain undone.**
Example **Her visit to the hairdressers was simply fiddling while Rome burned. Because she had much more important things to do today.**

Question: I would prefer that you did your homework tonight as its very important for your exam preparation. Don't you think?
Possible answer: No, I prefer to have my nails done. I don't consider that fiddling while Rome burns. Do you?

344).

TOOT, HORN, STRENGTHS

Idiom **Toot your own horn.**
Meaning **Means to talk about your own strengths.**
Example **He is always tooting his own horn.**

Question: How well do you think you are doing with your English?
Possible answer: Well if I do say so myself, I think my English is good. Is that tooting my own horn?

345).

BROKEN, RECORD, CONTINUALLY, POINT

Idiom **You sound like a broken record.**
Meaning **Someone who continually repeats himself.**
Example **You sound like a broken record. How many times are you going to say that?**

Question: You are starting to sound like a broken record. Do you have anything else to say.
Possible answer: Well I just want to get my point across to you.

346).

CHANGE, HEARING, RECORD

Idiom **Oh please, change the record.**
Meaning **Please talk about something else.**
Example **I wish he would change the record. I'm sick of hearing him say the same old thing.**
Question: You gave the same excuse last week. I wish you would change the record.
Possible answer: OK, I'm sorry but I don't have another excuse.

347).

HARPING, TALK, ELECTION, POLITICS, HATE, NEIGHBOUR

Idiom **Harping on.**
Meaning **To talk too much about something.**
Example **He is harping on about the election again. I hate politics.**

Question: What was he harping on about?
Possible answer: I don't know, something about his next door neighbour.

348).

MUSIC, EARS, PLEASED

Idiom **It was music to my ears.**
Meaning **Something to be pleased about.**
Example **When my son told me he got his new job, it was music to my ears.**

Question: Do you think you will pass your exam next week.
Possible answer: Well if I do, it will be music to my ears when I hear him say ¨you passed¨

349).

DRUM, UNDERSTANDS, REMEMBERED

Idiom **Drum something into your head.**
Meaning **To make sure someone understands the problem.**
Example **I had to really drum into his head so he remembered the phone number.**

Question: Are you good at remembering phone numbers?
Possible answer: Yes, but you really have to drum it into my head.

350).

CLOSING, CHEAPLY, QUID

Idiom **I got it for a song.**
Meaning **To get something really cheaply**
Example **I got the car for a song. Only five hundred quid.**

Question: How much was your new phone?
Possible answer: I got it for a song. They had a closing down sale at Apple.

Word translations.

Ring Badalar Understand Entender
Familiar Familiar Song Canção
Burn Queimar Cheap Chea
Horn Buzina Quid Libra
Broken Quebrado Record Gravação
Harping Falante / Expressivo Election Eleição
Drum Tamborilar Phone Telefonar

Please note that some of the translations are not literal. They are as close to the meaning of the idiom or the actual word as is possible.

Teaching Point

Practice the new words by repeating them over and over and ask the student to repeat the idiom by using the Tagging principle to prompt the student and then repeat together by using the Tandeming technique until the student can recite independently.

Sound & Music Idioms (2)

351).

COOKING, ADVENTURE,

Idiom **It rings my bell.**
Meaning **It makes me excited.**
Example **I'm very interested in that girl. She rings my bell.**

Question: What kind of things ring your bell.
Possible answer: A lot of things. I like fast cars, cooking, watching adventure movies etc.

352).

SUPPER, EXCHANGE, FAVOUR

Idiom **Sing for your supper.**
Meaning **To work in exchange for a favour.**
Example **If you want that new hat then you will have to sing for your supper. Wash my car for me please and I will buy it for you.**

Question: What does sing for your supper mean?
Possible answer: To work in exchange for something.

353).

FAT, ASSUME

Idiom **Not over till the fat lady sings.**
Meaning **Its not over until the final thing has happened.**
Example **Don't assume anything. Its not over until the fat lady sings.**

Question: You shouldn't leave a football game until the final whistle sounds should you?
Possible answer: No of course not, because its not over until the fat lady sings. Anything could still happen and surprise us all.

354).

WHISTLES, BELLS, ACCESSORY

Idiom **All the bells and whistles.**
Meaning **It has every accessory.**
Example **My new car has all the bells and whistles.**

Question: Does your car have all the bells and whistles?
Possible answer: No, its just a standard Fiat Uno.

355).

KNOCK, HURT, KNOCK, THREAT

Idiom **Knock seven bells out of him.**
Meaning **To really hurt someone.**
Example **My father said if I did that again he would knock seven bells out of me.**

Question: What does to knock seven bells out of someone mean.
Possible answer: It means to really hurt someone. Its a threat.

356).

MEANS, DRESS

Idiom **Whistle for it.**
Meaning **Means you can't have something.**
Example **No you can't have that new dress now. You can go and whistle for it.**

Question: If I said that you can go and whistle for something. What does it mean?
Possible answer: It means I can't have it.

357).

CLAPPERS

Idiom **Go like the clappers**
Meaning **To go very fast.**
Example **His new car goes like the clappers.**

Question: Is your motorbike very fast.
Possible answer: Yes, it goes like the clappers.

358).

SOUND, SWEET, PLEASANT, SERVICED

Idiom **To sound sweet.**
Meaning **Something pleasant to hear.**
Example **My car is sounding sweet at the moment. I just had it serviced.**

Question: Is your car running well at the moment?
Possible answer: Yes, I had it serviced last week and it sounds sweet.

359).

PURRING, KITTEN, SOUNDING, PURRS, PLEASANT

Idiom **Purring like a kitten.**
Meaning **Means that something is sounding very good.**
Example **My motorcycle purrs like a kitten at sixty miles per hour.**

Question: If I said that my scooter was purring like a kitten what would I mean?
Possible answer: Its sounds very pleasant and I running well.

360).

BARKING, DOUBTS

Idiom **Barking mad.**
Meaning **Means completely crazy.**
Example **He is barking mad if he thinks I will pay that.**

Question: Do you think I'm barking mad?
Possible answer: I have had my doubts about you for a long time.

End of lesson eighteen (Forty minutes)

Word translations.

Bell Sino Final Final Sweet Doce
Excited Animado Whistle Assobio Sound Som
Sing can'tar Accessory Acessorio Service Serviço
Supper Janter Knock Bater Purr Ronronar
Wash Lavagem Hurt Machucar Motorcycle moto
Car Carro Dress Vestido Barking Latido
Fat Gordura Clappers Rápido Mad Louco

Please note that some of the translations are not literal. They are as close to the meaning of the idiom or actual word as is possible.

End of lesson eighteen test

Below you will find a short test which covers the eighteenth and final lesson of this book. This short twenty minute test is meant as a revision and not as a marker for how well the student is progressing.

Tests all the way through these books are for motivational and revision purposes only. People perform differently under exam pressures and we believe that a student's primary aim is to learn a new skill and not to prove his or her worth. So, when giving the tests keep it light. The tests consist of ten yes or no questions and a short dictation containing some of the words introduced.

You will also find the answering sheets below. Please feel free to print off as many as needed for each student.

End of section dictation.

It didn't ring a bell when John reminded me about the party next week. I had completely forgotten about it. You do realise of course that guy is barking mad. I bought a new music system last week and it has all the bells and whistles you could ever need. I played my favourite CD on it and it sounded sweet. I was late for my dinner but my mother said I could whistle for it now. It had gone cold and it was now in the dog. She said if I'm late again, my dad would knock seven bells out of me. Anyway I went down the local cafe and ate there. You know what they say. It ain't over till the fat lady sings.

Ten questions about idioms.
Enter the missing words in the right hand column.

1 I can't remember. It doesn't seem to ring a _____.
2 You can go and sing for your ______.
3 Its not over you know until the ____ lady ____.
4 My new bike has all the _____ and _____.
5 My dad knocked seven _____ out of our neighbour.
6 Your dinner is in the dog. You can go and _____ for it now.
7 My motorbike sounds _____ now its had a service.
8 It purrs like a _____ now
9 That old guy is ______ mad
10 That scooter goes like the _____ with that 750cc engine in it.

Review the answers on the following page

Once the test is completed do a full review of all the errors and questions the student may have.

Test answers

1	Bell
2	Supper
3	Fat, Sings
4	Bells, Whistles
5	Bells
6	Whistle
7	Sweet
8	Kitten
9	Barking
10	Clappers

At this point in your studies do a full review of the previous sixty idioms in each of the previous three books before moving onto section seven The vocabulary content in these section will expand the student's ability to communicate greatly.

Lesson Nineteen

Music Idioms (4)

361).

MUSIC, PROBLEM, CONSEQUENCES,

Idiom **To face the music.**
Meaning **To face up to your problem and its consequences.**
Example **I had to go home and face the music.**

Question: If you were late home on a Saturday night when you were young. Did you dread going home and facing the music.
Possible answer: Yes, my dad was very strict with me. I hated have to face music.

362).

CHANGE, TUNE, OPINION

Idiom **To change your tune.**
Meaning **Means to change your opinion.**
Example **Well you have soon changed your tune.**

Question: You have soon changed your tune. You used to hate motorbikes.
Possible answer: Yes, I love them now.

363).

CHIME, INTERUPT, CONVERSATION DISCUSSION, IDEA

Idiom **To chime in.**
Meaning **To interrupt a conversation.**
Example **Just chime in when you feel like OK.**

Question: During the class discussion do you ever just chime in uninvited.
Possible answer: Yes, I thought that was the idea.

364).

STRUCK, CHORD, RELEVANT, STRIKE

Idiom **It struck a chord with me.**
Meaning **Means that when someone says something, it seems relevant to you. It has a meaning to you.**
Example **That struck a chord with me.**

Question: If I said I don't think you are doing enough home study. Would that strike a chord with you.
Possible answer: Yes, you are right, I realise that.

365).

SONG, DANCE, FUSS, IMPORTANT, BOTHERED

Idiom **Don't make a song and dance about it.**
Meaning **Means not to make a fuss about something.**
Example **OK, don't make a song and dance about it, its not that important.**

Question: When you were young did you ever make a song and dance about unimportant things.
Possible answer: Yes, all the time. But now I just can't be bothered.

366).

ELEVATOR, USUALLY, BORING, CENTRE, DEATH, COMPANY

Idiom **Elevator music.**
Meaning **Usually boring music.**
Example **I hate elevator music more than call centre music.**

Question: Have you ever got into a lift and been bored to death with the music in there?
Possible answer: There is only one thing worse than elevator music and that is being put on hold when calling your phone company.

367).

JAM, SESSION, IMPROMPTU, PLAYING, INSTRUMENT

Idiom **Having a jam session.**
Meaning **An impromptu session with people playing their instruments.**
Example **I love jamming.**

Question: Who sang a song called Jammin?
Possible answer: I think it was Bob Marley.

368).

JAZZ, FASTER, STRIPES

Idiom	**To jazz something up.**
Meaning	**To make something look better.**
Example	**I'm going to jazz up my car.**

Question: Have you jazzed up your car?
Possible answer: Yes, I put go faster stripes on it.

369).

TICKLE, IVORIES, PIANO, GRANDFATHER

Idiom	**To tickle the ivories.**
Meaning	**A funny way to say, I play the piano.**
Example	**My grandfather tickled the ivories.**

Question: Can you play the piano?
Possible answer: Yes, I've been tickling the ivories since I was a child.

370).

CALL, TUNE, DECISIONS, AROUND, ALTHOUGH

Idiom	**To call the tune.**
Meaning	**To make all the decisions.**
Example	**It seems like Mr. Jones calls the tune around here.**

Question: Who calls the tune in your house?
Possible answer: In reality, my mother. Although my dad thinks he does!

Word translations.

Tune Sintonia Boring tedioso
Opinion Opinião Jamming Improvisar
Chime Badalar Impromptu Improvisar
Conversation Conversação Instrument Instrumento
Chord acorde Tickle Agradar a
Struck bater Ivory Marfim
Dance dança
Fuss exagerar
Elevator elevador

Please note that some of the translations are not literal. They are as close to the meaning of the idiom or word as is possible.

Teaching Point

Practice the new words by repeating them over and over and ask the student to repeat the idiom by using the Tagging principle to prompt the student and then repeat together by using the Tandeming technique until the student can recite independently.

Body Idioms (1)

371).

STRONG, LAW, POWER, ARM, ARRESTED

Idiom	**Strong arm of the law.**
Meaning	**Meaning the power of the law.**
Example	**Here comes the strong arm of the law.**

Question: Have you ever felt the strong arm of the law.
Possible answer: Yes, I've been arrested many times.

372).

CHANCE, KNOWING, SUCCESS, DECIDED, DANGEROUS

Idiom	**To chance ones arm.**
Meaning	**To try something knowing that there is little chance of success.**
Example	**He decided to chance his arm anyway.**

Question: Would you take a chance and travel to a dangerous country.
Possible answer: Not at the moment I think it would be stupid to chance your arm in any Middle East country.

373).

COST, LOT, SYSTEM, BOUGHT, RECENTLY

Idiom	**It cost an arm and a leg.**
Meaning	**It cost a lot of money.**
Example	**My new music system cost an arm and a leg.**

Question: Have you bought anything recently that cost an arm and a leg?
Possible answer: Yes, my iPhone 5.

374).

RIGHT, ANYTHING, MOMENT, REST

Idiom	**To give your right arm for.**
Meaning	**Means you would give anything, well almost anything.**
Example	**I would give my right arm for a BMW 1200 GS**

Question: Would you give your right arm for anything at the moment?
Possible answer: Yes, a rest.

375).

FOOT, GRAVE, BOYFRIEND, MONEY

Idiom **One foot in the grave.**
Meaning **Very old.**
Example **He has one foot in the grave.**

Question: How old do you think her new boyfriend is?
Possible answer: He must have one foot in the grave. I think she is after his money.

376).

ANGRY, CONCERNED, BUILDING, NEIGHBOURS, POLITE

Idiom **Up in arms.**
Meaning **To be angry or very concerned about something.**
Example **He is up in arms about the building of the new road.**

Question: Do your neighbours ever get up in arms about how loud you play your music?
Possible answer: Oh yes, all the time. I turn it down if they ask me politely.

377).

LENGTH, SAFE, DISTANCE

Idiom **Keep at arms length.**
Meaning **To keep someone or something at a safe distance.**
Example **I always keep my neighbours at arms length.**

Question: Do you get on well with your neighbours?
Possible answer: Yes, but I like to keep them at arms length.

378).

ASKING, WISHING, POWER, ENCOURAGEMENT, ELBOW

Idiom **More power to your elbow.**
Meaning **To give someone encouragement.**
Example **More power to your elbow my friend. I hope you succeed.**

Question: Did you manage to get that new job?
Possible answer: Yes, I did. Thanks for asking and wishing me more power to my elbow last week.

379).

GREASE, MIGHT, ENOUGH, STUDIES

Idiom **To use elbow grease.**
Meaning **To work hard.**
Example **Put a little more elbow grease into it and you might be able to lift that piano.**

Question: Do you think you should put a little more elbow grease into your studies?
Possible answer: Well I already study two hours every day. Don't you think that's enough?

380).

CLASSROOM, OVERCROWDED, AGREE

Idiom **Elbow room.**
Meaning **Not enough room. I need some more.**
Example **There isn't enough elbow room in here.**

Question: We need a little more elbow room in this classroom. Its starting to be overcrowded.
Possible answer: Yes, I agree its too small.

Word translations.

Arm Braço ˊ Building Construção
Law Lei Neighbour Vizinho
Power Poder Length Distancia
Chance Chance Safe Seguro
Anyway de qualquer maneira Elbow Cotovelo
Cost Custo Encourage Encorajar
System Sistema Succeed Suceder
Grave Tumulo Grease Graxa
Concern Preocupação Lift Levantar

Please note that some of the translations are not literal. They are as close too the meaning of the idiom or word as is possible.

End of lesson nineteen (Forty minutes)

End of lesson nineteen test

Below you will find a short test which covers the lesson above. This short twenty minute test is meant as a revision and not as a marker for how well the student is progressing.

Tests all the way through these books are for motivational and revision purposes only. People perform differently under exam pressures and we believe that a student's primary aim is to learn a new skill and not to prove his or her worth. So, when giving the tests keep it light. The tests consist of ten simple questions and a short dictation containing some of the words introduced. You will also find the answering sheets and answer sheets below. Please feel free to print off as many as needed for each of your students.

End of lesson nineteen dictation

I bought a lovely forty two inch LCD television two months ago and it cost an arm and a leg, but last night someone broke into my apartment and stole it. All the neighbours are up in arms because the thieves made a mess and damaged the garden fence. The old guy next door has one foot in the grave and would find it difficult to defend himself if they broke into his apartment. We decided to strengthen our security systems just in case they returned. With any luck though, the police will catch them and the thieves will feel the strong arm of the law. The strengthened security systems have now been jazzed up and we all feel safer. All it took was a little elbow grease and we finished the work in no time at all.

Ten questions about idioms.
Enter the missing words in the right hand column.

1 Strong arm of the ______.
2 It _____ and arm and a _____.
3 I would give my _____ arm for one of those.
4 The old guy living next door has ____ foot in the _____.
5 All the family are ____ in arms about the changes.
6 I keep my girlfriend at arms ______ now. She was crazy.
7 I say, more ______ to your elbow. Good luck.
8 All you have to do is put a little more _____ grease into it.
9 We need a little more _____ room to work.
10 My grandfather loves to _____ the ivories.

Review the answers on the following page

Once the test is completed do a full review of all the errors and questions the student may have.

Test Answers

1	Law
2	Cost, Leg
3	Right
4	One, Grave
5	Up
6	Length
7	Power
8	Elbow
9	Elbow
10	Tickle

Lesson Twenty

Body Idioms (2)

381).

BREAK, BACK, STAIRS, SOUNDS, POUNDS, COURSE

Idiom **Break your back**
Meaning **Means to work too hard.**
Example **I'm not going to break my back for you getting that piano up the stairs.**

Question: Would you break your back for five pounds an hour?
Possible answer: No of course not. That sounds like slave labour.

382).

BELLY, FAILED, WINDOW, CLEANING, STARTED, SUCCESS

Idiom **Go belly up.**
Meaning **A business or idea that failed.**
Example **I started a window cleaning business but it went belly up after six months.**

Question: If you started a business would you let it go belly up.
Possible answer: No, I would try my best to make a success of it.

383).

STAB, BETRAY, TRUST, STABBERS, ANOTHER, THROUGH

Idiom **To stab someone in the back.**
Meaning **Means to say something bad about someone or to betray their trust.**
Example **I hate back stabbers. Don't you?**

Question: Has anyone you trusted ever stabbed you in the back?
Possible answer: Yes, I had a friend who said unkind things about me. I found out through another friend.

384).

WALL, SERIOUS, DIFFICULTIES, SOLVE, FINANCIALLY, DECIDED, BANKRUPT

Idiom **To have your back to the wall.**
Meaning **You have serious difficulties and can't solve them.**
Example **I had my back to the wall financially and eventually decided to declare myself bankrupt.**

Question: Have you ever found yourself with your back to the wall?
Possible answer: Yes about three years ago. I ran out of money after being made redundant.

385).

CAT, IRON, STOMACH, DIGESTIVE, SYSTEM, FOODS, UPSET

Idiom **I have a cast iron stomach**
Meaning **Very strong digestive system.**
Example **I can eat anything.**

Question: Do you like all foods?
Possible answer: Yes most things. I can eat anything. My stomach never gets upset. Its cast iron.

386).

DEAD, BODY, REFUSE, AMOUNT, PEAS, DOUBLE, CLASSES

Idiom **Over my dead body.**
Meaning **To refuse to do something.**
Example **I wont pay that amount for a tin of peas. Over my dead body.**

Question: Is it OK if I double your tuition fees for the English classes.
Possible answer: Over my dead body!

387).

BLOOD, BOIL, ANGRY, LOUD, HONESTLY, RUDE, TRASPORT

Idiom **It makes my blood boil.**
Meaning **To make me very angry.**
Example **Honestly, that loud music is making my blood boil.**

Question: What kind of things make your blood boil?
Possible answer: Rude people on public transport make my blood boil.

388).

SWEAT, TEARS, LOT, EXAM, EASILY

Idiom **Blood, sweat and tears.**
Meaning **Something that takes a lot of effort.**
Example **I put blood, sweat and tears into building that business.**

Question: Do you study English a lot?
Possible answer: Only blood sweat and tears. So I should pass the exam easily.

389).

BAG, BONES, THIN, DIETING

Idiom **A bag of bones.**
Meaning **Someone who is very thin.**
Example **She is a bag of bones.**

Question: Have you been dieting again?
Possible answer: Yes why? Do I look like a bag of bones again?

390).

COLD, SCARES, ACCIDENT, YESTERDAY

Idiom **Makes my blood run cold.**
Meaning **Something that scares you.**
Example **That accident yesterday made my blood run cold.**

Question: Have you ever seen anything that made your blood run cold?
Possible answer: Yes, that accident yesterday.

Word table with translations.

Belly Estomago Bankrupt Falido Honest Honesto
Fail Falhar / Faltar Cast Iron Ferro Fundido Bones Ossos
Cleaning Limpeza Digestive Digestivo Run Corrida
Stab Apunhalar Dead Morto Scare Susto
Trust Confiar em Refuse Recusar
Betray Trair Tin Estanho/ Lata
Serious Sério Peas Ervilhas
Solve Resolver Boil Ferver/ Cozinhar
Declare Declarar Blood Sangue

Please note that some translations are not literal. They are as close to the meaning of the idiom and word as is possible.

Teaching Point

Practice the new words by repeating them over and over and ask the student to repeat the idioms by using the Tagging principle to prompt the student and then repeat together by using the Tandeming technique until the student can recite independently.

Body Idioms (3)

391).

FINGERS, STUDYING

Idiom **Work my your fingers to the bone.**
Meaning **Working very hard.**
Example **I worked my fingers to my bone yesterday.**

Question: Do you work your fingers to the bone studying?
Possible answer: Yes every night.

392).

CONTENTION, DISAGREEMENT, VALIDITY

Idiom **A bone of contention**
Meaning **A subject with a lot of disagreement.**
Example **Its a bone of contention with him. He doesn't agree at all.**

Question: Are exams a bone of contention with you?
Possible answer: Yes, I'm not sure I agree with there validity.

393).

HESITATE, SUBJECT

Idiom **Make no bones about it.**
Meaning **I don't hesitate to say something about a subject.**
Example **Make no bones about it, I don't agree.**

Question: Make no bones about it, I expect you to pass your exam.
Possible answer: I will do my best.

394).

THROW, REWARD, MOTIVATE, FINISH, TASK, EXPECT, PAY

Idiom **To throw someone a bone.**
Meaning **To give a reward to motivate someone.**
Example **Throw him a bone. It will motivate him to finish the task.**

Question: If you work hard with your studies, I will throw you a bone as a reward.
Possible answer: I don't expect you to pay me all the money before I finish the job for you, but if the could just throw me a small bone it would help.

395).

HEAD, AROUND, UNDERSTAND, EITHER

Idiom **Get your head around something.**
Meaning **To understand something.**
Example **Wait, I need to get my head around this.**

Question: I can't get my head around why he did that. Do you know why?
Possible answer: No, I can't get my head around it either.

396).

NO-BRAINER, OPTION, OBVIOUS, EASY

Idiom **This is a no-brainer.**
Meaning **The option is obvious.**
Example **Its a no-brainer. The car is so cheap, you have to buy it.**

Question: Passing your exams is simply a no-brainer. Don't you think?
Possible answer: If all goes well it should be easy for me.

397)

BRAINS, PICK, ADVICE, FIXING

Idiom **Pick my brains.**
Meaning **Ask someone for advice.**
Example **Can I pick your brains about fixing my TV.**

Question: If you don't understand one of the questions you can pick my brains.
Possible answer: OK, great.

398).

BRAWN, STRONG, INTELLIGENCE, IDIOT, GYM, LIBRARY

Idiom **All brawn and no brains.**
Meaning **Physically strong but no intelligence.**
Example **What an idiot. All brawn and no brains.**

Question: Your new boyfriend is all brawn and no brains. Too much time spent in the gym and not in the library.
Possible answer: He is not my boyfriend. He is my personal trainer.

399).

BEAT, UNDERSTAND,DIFFICULT, IMPORTANT, WORRIED

Idiom	**Don't beat your brains out.**
Meaning	**Trying to understand something but finding it difficult.**
Example	**Don't beat your brains out Phil its really not that important.**

Question: Listen, if you don't pass your driving test the first time you can always do it again. So don't beat your brains out.
Possible answer: Yes I know. I'm not worried.

400).

MEMORY, SIEVE, HONESTLY

Idiom	**Memory like a sieve.**
Meaning	**A very bad memory.**
Example	**My wife has a brain like a sieve.**

Question: Did you find your keys?
Possible answer: Yes, I had left them in the door. Honestly, I have a memory like a sieve.

Word translations.

Contention Contenção Advice Conselho
Disagreement Desacordo Brawn Musculo
Hesitate Hesitar Beat Bater
Throw Jogar Sieve Peneira
Motivate Motivar Memory Memoria
Reward Recompensa
Finish Fim
No-brainer Simples
Pick Escolher
Fix Fixar

Please note that some of the translations are not literal. They are as close to the meaning of the idiom or actual word as is possible.

End of lesson Twenty (Forty minutes)

End of lesson test

Below you will find a short test which covers the twentieth lesson idioms. This short twenty minute test is meant as a revision and not as a marker for how well the student is progressing. Tests all the way through these books are for motivational and revision purposes only. People perform differently under exam pressures and we believe that a student's primary aim is to learn a new skill and not to prove his or her worth.

So, when giving the tests keep it light.

The tests consist of ten questions and a short dictation containing some of the words introduced.

You will also find the answering sheets and answer sheets below. Please feel free to print off as many as needed for each student.

End of lesson twenty dictation

Just lately I have been working my fingers to the bone and make no bones about it, I am hoping it pays off. I have been trying to get my head around a problem that has been bothering me for a while now. Firstly, I tried to pick my brothers brains because I thought he was an expert, but it turned out that he knew less than I did. I remember an old friend telling me that he had faced the same problem some years ago, but I have been beating my brains trying to remember his name. Just lately, I really have got a memory like a sieve. It should be a no-brainer but I just could not get my head around it. If only someone could throw me a bone, maybe, just maybe I could remember the guys name.

Ten questions about idioms.
Enter the missing words in the right hand column.

1 I have been working my _____ to the bone all week.
2 I have a ______ of contention with this problem.
3 Lets make no _______ about this. I have made up my mind.
4 I am getting a little impatient now. At least ______ me a bone.
5 Wait a moment, let me get my _____ around this before we make any decisions.
6 Really this is a ___ brainer if you think about it.
7 Can I _____ your brains about what its like in Brazil?
8 Your boyfriend is all brawn and no _____.
9 Don't beat your ______ out about it. It will be alright on the night.
10 Honestly Rose, you have a memory like a _______.

Review the answers on the following page

Once the test is completed do a full review of all the errors and questions the student may have.

It's important to note that each book carries the same introduction and instruction as the first book. This is so that any stage of instruction can be bought if your student has a higher level of English than a complete beginner. You can buy a stage four book and still learn about the method of teaching without buying the whole series.

Test Answers

1	Fingers
2	Bone
3	Bones
4	Throw
5	Head
6	No
7	Pick
8	Brains
9	Brains
10	Sieve

Lesson Twenty One

Each section in this e-book contains twenty English idioms with explanations. As with the other e-books in this method the student repeats the idiom until the pronunciation is correct and the meaning is understood. Where possible the Portuguese equivalent is compared alongside. Each e-book contains sixty idioms and a short self-test at the end.

Body Idioms (4)

401).

PLAY, EAR, PREPARATION, FATE, ADVENTURE, PACKAGE, HOLIDAY

Idiom Play it by ear.
Meaning To do something without much preparation.
Example Lets just play it by ear and see where fate takes us.

Question: When you go on holiday, do you usually play it by ear and hope for adventure? Or are you more of a package holiday person?
Possible answer: I usually like a bit of adventure.

402)

GRIN, BEAR, UNCOMFORTABLE, SPRING, WINTER, WEATHER, IMPROVES

Idiom To grin and bear it.
Meaning To put up with something a little uncomfortable.
Example It wont be long until spring. Winter is nearly over. We will just have to grin and bear it for now.

Question: Do you like winter?
Possible answer: Well its just a matter of grinning and bearing it until the weather improves.

403).

MUSIC, LOVING, HEAR, MARRIED, STAGE, EXAM

Idiom **Its music to my ears.**
Meaning **Something I am loving to hear.**
Example **It was music to my ears when I heard she was getting married.**

Question: If I told you, you had passed your stage seven English exam. How would you feel?
Possible answer: It would be music to my ears.

404).

TURN, DEAF, DELIBERATELY, THOUGHT, PROBABLY, TURN, MOMENT

Idiom **To turn a deaf ear.**
Meaning **To deliberately not listen to what was said.**
Example **If I thought you were cheating I would probably turn a deaf ear.**

Question: If I told you I knew where the robbers were hiding what would you do?
Possible answer: I would probably a turn a deaf ear. I have enough problems to deal with at the moment.

405).

BLIND, EYE, DELIBERATELY, CHEATING, TURN

Idiom **Turn a blind eye.**
Meaning **Not to look at something deliberately. To ignore.**
Example **I'm going to turn a blind eye this time.**

Question: If I saw you cheating in an exam, what do you think I should do?
Possible answer: Well, I would hope you would turn a blind eye.

406).

BURN, BEHIND, BURNING

Idiom **To make ones ears burn.**
Meaning **To talk about someone behind their backs.**
Example **I knew something was going on. My ears were burning.**

Question: Were your ears burning the other day? I was talking about you to your mother.
Possible answer: Yes. What did you say?

407).

CLIP, AROUND, SHARP, NAUGHTY

Idiom **Give someone a clip around the ear.**
Meaning **A short sharp slap on the side of the head.**
Example **My dad was always giving me a clip around the ear.**

Question: Did your dad ever give you a clip around the ear when you were young?
Possible answer: Yes, all the time if was naughty.

408).

EARFUL, ANGRY, DAUGHTER

Idiom To give someone an earful.
Meaning To tell someone what you think about them. Be angry with them.
Example I will give him an earful when I get home.

Question: When was the last time you gave your daughter an earful?
Possible answer: This morning. She wouldn't get out of bed.

409).

IMPRESSED, CONGRATULATIONS, PASSED

Idiom Got to hand it to you.
Meaning Means that I am impressed with what you did or said.
Example I've got to hand it to you girl. Well done.

Question: Congratulations you passed easily. I've got to hand it to you. I'm impressed.
Possible answer: Thanks.

410).

LOOKING, GROUND, LISTENING

Idiom Keep an ear to the ground
Meaning To be listening out for something.
Example I will keep my ear to the ground about a new car for you.

Question: Will you keep your ear to the ground. I'm looking for a new job.
Possible answer: Yes sure. What kind of work are you looking for?

Word translations.

Fat Gordura Clip Acertar
Preparation Preparação Sharp Forte / Afiado
Grin Sorriso Angry Zangado / Irritado
Winter Inverno Earful Ouvido / Completo
Deaf Surdo Hand (give) Dar / Presentear
Deliberate Deliberado
Blind Cego
Ignore Ignorar
Behind Atras
Burn Queimar

Please note that some of the translations are not literal. They are as close to the meaning of the idiom or the actual word as is possible.

Teaching Point

Practice the new words by repeating them over and over and ask the student to repeat the idiom by using the Tagging principle to prompt the student and then repeat together by using the Tandeming technique until the student can recite independently.

Body Idioms (5)

411).

LEND, LISTEN, CAESAR, COUNTRYMEN, FRIENDS

Idiom **Lend me an ear.**
Meaning **Listen to what I have to say.**
Example **Can you lend me your ear just for one moment?**

Question: What was it Julius Caesar said?
Possible answer: Friends, Romans, Countrymen, lend me your ears

412).

APPLE, FAVOURITE, YOUNGEST

Idiom **She is the apple of my eye.**
Meaning **My favourite person.**
Example **My daughter is the apple of my eye.**

Question: Who is the apple of your eye?
Possible answer: My youngest son, he is only six months old.

413).

BAT, EYELID, SURPRISED, NOTICE, PAYING, NAKED

Idiom **Not to bat an eyelid.**
Meaning **Means not to be surprised at all. Not to notice.**
Example **He didn't bat an eyelid when that young guy walked out of the shop without paying for the CD.**

Question: If someone ran down the street naked what would you do?
Possible answer: To be honest, I wouldn't bat an eyelid.

414).

ESPECIALLY, RAISE, EYEBROWS, SURPRISED, EXPRESSION, WALKING

Idiom **To raise someone's eyebrows.**
Meaning **To be surprised. Its an expression on ones face.**
Example **He ran down the street naked and it raised a few eyebrows I can tell you.**

Question: If you saw someone walking down the street in her bikini, what do you think would happen?
Possible answer: Well at the very least it would raise a few eyebrows. Especially in winter.

415).

WIDE, FULLY, AWARE, RESPONSIBILITY, CONTRACT

Idiom **Eyes wide open.**
Meaning **To be fully aware of what you are doing or what is happening around you.**
Example **I took the responsibility of the job with my eyes wide open.**

Question: You must always go into a contract with your eyes wide open.
Possible answer: Yes I know.

416).

HAWK, SIGHT, EVERYTHING, MILES

Idiom **Eyes like a hawk.**
Meaning **To have very good sight.**
Example **He saw everything. He must have eyes like a hawk.**

Question: Did you notice the guy parachuting into the soccer ground this morning?
Possible answer: You must have eyes like a hawk, its over ten miles away from here.

417).

FEAST, CHRISTMAS

Idiom **Feast you eyes on that.**
Meaning **Means to take a really good look at something.**
Example **Feast your eyes on that Christmas dinner.**

Question: If I said, feast your eyes on that. What would I mean?
Possible answer: You would mean, have a really good look.

418).

EAGLE, SHARP, EYESIGHT, HAYSTACK

Idiom **Eagle eyes.**
Meaning **To have very sharp (good) sight.**
Example **Your eyesight must be very good, I can't see it.**

Question: Heh, eagle eyes, can you find that needle in a haystack for me please?
Possible answer: My eyesight isn't that good, sorry.

419).

BEFORE, CLEARLY, DISAPPEAR

Idiom **Before your very eyes.**
Meaning **Someone will do something in front of you, so you can see it clearly.**
Example **I will make it disappear right before your very eyes.**

Question: If I disappeared right before your very eyes, how would you feel?
Possible answer: At the moment, happy.

420).

FULLY, NEVER, GLAD, DIVORCE, PROBABLY

Idiom	**To see eye to eye.**
Meaning	**To fully agree with someone about something.**
Example	**We never saw eye to eye anyway. I'm glad about the divorce.**

Question: Do you see eye to eye with me about politics?
Possible answer: Probably not. I'm a Liberal.

End of lesson twenty one (Forty minutes)

Word translations.

Lend Emprestar Eyebrow Sobrancelha Eyesight Visão
Listen Ouvir Raise Levantar Disappear Desaparecer
Apple Maça Hawk Falcão Divorce Divorcio
Favourite Favorito Feast Festa / Banquete
Bat Morcego Christmas Natal
Eyelid Palpebra Eagle Aguia
Young Jovem Sharp Forte

Please note that some of the translations are not literal. They are as close to the meaning of the idiom or actual word as is possible.

End of lesson twenty one test

Below you will find a short test which covers the twenty one and final lesson of this book. This short twenty minute test is meant as a revision and not as a marker for how well the student is progressing.

Tests all the way through these books are for motivational and revision purposes only. People perform differently under exam pressures and we believe that a student's primary aim is to learn a new skill and not to prove his or her worth. So, when giving the tests keep it light. The tests consist of ten yes or no questions and a short dictation containing some of the words introduced.

You will also find the answering sheets below. Please feel free to print off as many as needed for each student.

End of section dictation.

My father and I never really saw eye to eye about things, I guess it was the age difference mainly. Although, many of the things I did as a teenager he never batted an eyelid. When I did do something wrong it was as though he had eyes like a hawk. He never missed a trick. I have started to learn how to be a magician. ¨Not like this like that¨ is my motto. Yesterday, a young woman walked past our office and I said to my friend, just feast your eyes on her. She was truly beautiful. She was wearing a very short skirt and nobody in the street really raised an eyebrow, except of course for me.

Ten questions about idioms.
Enter the missing words in the right hand column.

1 Friends, Romans and Countrymen, lend me your _____.
2 She really is the ______ of you eye isn't she?
3 He didn't bat an ______ when I left work early today.
4 She raised a few_______ when she walked passed the building site.
5 I always go into agreements with my _____ wide _____.
6 Wow, you must have eyes like a ______.
7 Feast your ______ on that for a Sunday lunch.
8 How can you see that far. You must have _____eyes.
9 I'm going to make her disappear right before ______ very eyes.
10 My father and I never saw _____ to _____.

Review the answers on the following page
Once the test is completed do a full review of all the errors and questions the student may have.

Test answers

1	Ears
2	Apple
3	Eyelid
4	Eyebrows
5	Eyes, Open
6	Hawk
7	Eyes
8	Eagle
9	Your
10	Eye, Eye

At this point in your studies do a full review of the previous sixty idioms in each of the previous three sections before moving onto section eight The vocabulary content in these sections will expand the student's ability to communicate greatly.

Lesson Twenty-Two

Random Idioms (1)

421).

WORD, MIDDLE, TROUBLE, STORM, FOUND, EYE, HIMSELF

Idiom **In the eye of the storm**
Meaning **To be in the middle of a lot of trouble.**
Example **He found himself in the eye of the storm this morning.**

Question: Have you ever found yourself in the eye of a storm?
Possible answer: Yes, my mother and father were arguing yesterday and I ended up right in the middle of it.

422).

MIND, EYE, THINKING, FRONT

Idiom **In your minds eye**
Meaning **Something at the front of mind.**
Example **I have been thinking about you all day. You are in my minds eye.**

Question: In your minds eye who is the best English actress at the moment?
Possible answer: I think Helen Mirren is wonderful.

423).

BLINK, TWINKLE, FINISHED, QUICKLY, GONE

Idiom **In the blink of an eye.**
Meaning **Gone quickly, finished very quickly.**
Example **In a twinkle of the eye the UFO had gone.**

Question: Did you see that?
Possible answer: Yes but it was gone in the blink of an eye.

424).

BORN, RIDING, ENOUGH, OLD, DAUGHTER, BORN

Idiom	**A twinkle in your eye**
Meaning	**Before your son or daughter was born.**
Example	**When you were just a twinkle in my eye I was riding motorcycles.**

Question: How old are you?
Possible answer: Old enough to be your mother. I was riding motorcycles when you were just a twinkle in your fathers eye.

425).

SITUATION, ACCIDENT, MOTIVE

Idiom	**More than meets the eye.**
Meaning	**More to the situation than you can see.**
Example	**There is more to this than meets the eye.**

Question: There is more to this accident than meets the eye!
Possible answer: I think so too. I think he had a motive.

426).

INSULT, NEGATIVE, RETURN, DESERVE

Idiom	**One in the eye**
Meaning	**To return an insult of negative to someone.**
Example	**That's one in the eye for him.**

Question: If I said that's one in the eye for him. What would I mean?
Possible answer: You would mean that he deserves what has happened to him.

427).

STRAIGHT, PROBLEM, TALK

Idiom	**To face something face to face**
Meaning	**Look at a problem straight away. Face a problem.**
Example	**I need to talk to him, face to face.**

Question: What does face to face mean?
Possible answer: It means to face your problem and deal with it.

428).

FACE OFF, BOXING, TONIGHT, RIDICULOUS, GUY, MATCH

Idiom	**Face off**
Meaning	**To meet something head on.**
Example	**Tonight there will be a boxing match. They will face off.**

Question: I need to have a face off with the guy next door. His music is ridiculously high.
Possible answer: I would be careful if I was you he's about six foot six.

429).

FACE VALUE, WORTH, ACCEPT, DEPENDS, PEOPLE

Idiom **On face value**
Meaning **To take something for what it is worth.**
Example **I have to accept this for what it is. On face value.**

Question: Do you agree that you should take people on face value?
Possible answer: It depends. I don't like to judge people until I get to know them.

430).

BRAVE, HAPPENING, FAIL, BANKRUPTCY, PUTTING

Idiom **A brave face on it.**
Meaning **To act brave about something that is happening to you.**
Example **He put a brave face on the things while he was going through the bankruptcy.**

Question: Are you upset that you failed your driving test?
Possible answer: Yes, but I'm putting a brave face on it.

Word table with translations.

Storm	Tempestade	Boxing	Boxe
Trouble	Dificildade	Accept	Aceitar
Mind	Mente	Value	Valor
Blink	Piscar	Brave	Bravo
Twinkle	Brilhar	Happen	Acontecer
Ride	Andar	Fail	Falhar
Situation	Situação	Test	Teste
Insult	Insultar	Act	Ato
Negative	Negativo	Worth	Valor
Straight	Em Linha reta	Head on	Bater de frente

Please note that some of the translations are not literal. They are as close to the meaning of the idiom or word as is possible.

Teaching Point

Practice the new words by repeating them over and over and ask the student to repeat the idiom by using the Tagging principle to prompt the student and then repeat together by using the Tandeming technique until the student can recite independently.

Head & Face Idioms (1)

431).

CHIN, ACCEPT, EXPERIENCE, BOSS, NEGATIVE, HAPPENED

Idiom **Take on the chin**
Meaning **To accept something negative that happened to you.**
Example **I took in on the chin and put it down to experience.**

Question: My boss got very angry this morning. I nearly lost my job arguing with him. What would you have done?

Possible answer: I´d have taken it on the chin especially if I was in the wrong.

432).

COMPANY, OWNER, ACCEPTED, TRYING, GIRLFRIEND

Idiom **Get a foot in the door**
Meaning **Trying to be accepted.**
Example **Her boyfriend is trying to get one foot in the door with his girlfriends family.**

Question: I really want to work for that new company.
Possible answer: So try and get to know the owner and get a foot in the door.
433).

RECOVERING, SERIOUS, FINANCIAL, REALISE, GETTING

Idiom **Back on your feet**
Meaning **After some serious problems. Financial or health. Recovering from.**
Example **I'm just getting back on my feet after my operation.**

Question: Do you realise that I have I recently returned to work after a long illness.
Possible answer: I'm glad to know you are getting back on your feet.

434).

DRAG, THOUGHT, SLOW, TOOK

Idiom **Drag your feet**
Meaning **To go too slow.**
Example **Come on son, stop dragging your feet.**

Question: Did I tell you that took my son out on a very long walk last Sunday?
Possible answer: I thought he is only five years old. Did he drag his feet?

435).

COMFORTABLE, STARTING

Idiom **Find your feet**
Meaning **To start to feet comfortable with something.**
Example **I am just starting to find my feet working here.**

Question: I understand you have just started a new job. How is it going?
Possible answer: I'm just finding my feet. But I'm sure its going to be great.

436).

ITCHY, IMMIGATE, REALISE, FEELING, SCHOOL

Idiom **Itchy feet.**
Meaning **Feeling like you need a change.**
Example **I have itchy feet. Think I will immigrate to Australia.**

Question: I'm thinking of moving to a new school. What do you think?
Possible answer: I didn't realise you had itchy feet.

437).

WET, IDEA, DRAW, ART

Idiom **Get your feet wet**
Meaning **To start something new.**
Example **I have only just started running but I will get my feet wet in a 10k run next Sunday.**

Question: I'm going to start going to an art class at the local college. What do you think of my idea?
Possible answer: You can draw me if you want, just to get your feet wet.

438).

WORLD, OPPORTUNITY, SUCCEED, JOIN, SURPRISED

Idiom **World at your feet**
Meaning **Have every opportunity to succeed in life when you are young.**
Example **He has the world at his feet. I'm not surprised he has joined the Army.**

Question: Did you know that my sister is immigrating to Australia next month?
Possible answer: I don't blame. She is only twenty two years old. She has the world at her feet.

439).

GROUND, SENSIBLE, STAY, DREAMING

Idiom	**Keep your feet on the ground**
Meaning	**To stay sensible.**
Example	**I just won the lottery but I will keep my feet on the ground.**

Question: If you won the lottery this Saturday, would you be able to keep your feet on the ground?
Possible answer: Probably not. I've already spent most of it just dreaming about it.

440).

RUSHED, BUSY, MOMENT

Idiom	**Rushed off your feet**
Meaning	**Very busy.**
Example	**I am rushed off my feet. So busy today.**

Question: Will you go to the cinema with me next Saturday night?
Possible answer: Sorry I can't. I'm rushed off my feet at the moment.

Word translations.

Chin Queixo Wet Molhado
Boss Chefe College Faculdade
Trying Tentando World Mundo
Company Companhia Army Exército
Serious Serio Join Juntar
Recover Recuperação Ground Terreno
Drag Arrasto Sensible Sensato
Comfortable Confortável Rush Apressar
Itchy Que Faz Comichão Busy Ocupado
Immigrate Imigração Dream Sonhar

Please note that some of the translations are not literal. They are as close too the meaning of the idiom or word as is possible.

End of lesson twenty-two (Forty minutes)

It's important at this point to review all of the words and idioms one more time before moving onto lesson number twenty three. Once the student is comfortable, then it's safe to move forward.

End of lesson Twenty-two test

Below you will find a short test which covers the lesson above. This short twenty minute test is meant as a revision and not as a marker for how well the student is progressing.

Tests all the way through these books are for motivational and revision purposes only. People perform differently under exam pressures and we believe that a student's primary aim is to learn a new skill and not to prove his or her worth. So, when giving the tests keep it light. The tests consist of ten simple questions and a short dictation containing some of the words introduced. You will also find the answering sheets and answer sheets below. Please feel free to print off as many as needed for each of your students.

End of lesson twenty-two dictation

I found myself in the eye of the storm this morning when my mother and father began to argue about what has happened to my younger brother. In the blink of an eye the car came around the corner and knocked him to the ground. I know they are putting a brave face on things and are very worried about him now. However, I am sure once he is out of hospital he will soon be back on his feet. When he is ready to return to work I think he should try to get one foot in the door with that new company that has opened up down the road. The salary will be much higher than what he receives now. I think what his manager said to him last week was fair about his continued lateness and he should just take it on the chin and move on.

Ten questions about idioms.
Enter the missing words in the right hand column.

1. In the ______ of the storm.
2. In you ______ eye.
3. He was just a ________ in my eye.
4. It was _____ in a twinkle of the _______.
5. There is more to this than ______ the eye.
6. I know he is putting a _______ face on it.
7. I am going to take him on ______ value.
8. You will just have to take it on the ____.
9. You need to try and get a _____ in the door.
10. I hope he gets back _____ his _____ soon.

Review the answers on the following page

Once the test is completed do a full review of all the errors and questions the student may have.

It's important to note that all ten books carry the same introduction and instruction as the first book. This is so that any stage of instruction can be bought and used independently. If your student has a higher level of English than a complete beginner then you can simply purchase the higher level books.

You can buy a stage four book and still learn about the method of teaching without buying the whole series.

Test Answers

1	Eye
2	Minds
3	Twinkle
4	Gone, Twinkle
5	Meets
6	Brave
7	Face
8	Chin
9	Foot
10	On, Feet

Lesson Twenty-Three

Each section contains twenty English idioms with meaning and examples. The student repeats the idiom until the pronunciation is correct and the meaning is understood. Where possible the Portuguese equivalent is compared alongside. Each section contains sixty idioms and a short self-test at the end.

Foot Idioms (2)

441).

STAND, INDEPENDENT, ENOUGH, OWN, LEFT

Idiom **Stand on your own two feet**
Meaning **To be independent**
Example **He is old enough to stand on his own two feet now.**

Question: How old were you when you left home to live on your own?
Possible answer: I was ready to stand on my own two feet when I was eighteen years old.

442).

THINK, DECISIONS, PLAN, SPENT, SPECIAL AIR SERVICE

Idiom **To think on your feet**
Meaning **To think while you are working or while something is happening. To make decisions when needed.**
Example **We had to think on out feet. We didn't have a plan.**

Question: Are you good at thinking on your feet?
Possible answer: Yes I spent six years in the Special Air Service (SAS) we had to.

443).

DANCE, LEFT

Idiom **Two left feet**
Meaning **can't dance!**
Example **I've got two left feet.**

Question: Can you dance?
Possible answer: No, I've got two left feet.

444).

BEST, WHILE, LETS, NERVOUS, INTERVIEW

Idiom **Best foot forward**
Meaning **To give your best while doing something.**
Example **Put your best foot forward and lets do this.**

Question: Are you nervous about the job interview tomorrow?
Possible answer: A little. My father told me to just put my best foot forward and I would be fine.

445).

PUTTING, HAPPENING, STAYING

Idiom **Put your foot down**
Meaning **To stop something happening firmly.**
Example **I had to put my foot down and say no.**

Question: Did you talk to your daughter about staying out too late on Saturday nights?
Possible answer: Yes, I'm putting my foot down. She wont be doing it again.

446).

FOOTLOOSE, FANCY, ANYTHING, ELDEST

Idiom **Foot loose and fancy free.**
Meaning **To be free to do anything I want.**
Example **Leave him alone, he's footloose and fancy free.**

Question: How old is your eldest son now?
Possible answer: He is twenty one years old. Footloose and fancy free.

447).

SHOULDN´T, HAPPY, REALLY, SPEAKING

Idiom **Put your foot in it.**
Meaning **To say something you shouldn't have.**
Example **I put my foot in it and now she knows. She isn't happy.**

Question: What did you say to her. He is very upset.
Possible answer: I really put my foot in it and now he isnt speaking to me.

448).

WRONG, MISTAKES, EXAM, HARDLY

Idiom **To put a foot wrong.**
Meaning **Make no mistakes.**
Example **He didn't put a foot wrong in his driving test.**

Question: He did very well in his exam last week.
Possible answer: Yes I know he hardly put a foot wrong.

449).

SHOE, OTHER, WOULDN´T, STUPID, IDEA

Idiom **Shoe on the other foot**
Meaning **Means that it was happening to you and not me.**
Example **If the show was on the other foot you wouldn't say that.**

Question: Told him not to do it, its a stupid idea. What would you have done?
Possible answer: If the shoe was on the other foot I would have done the same.

450).

SHOOT, NEGATIVE, EFFECT, TRUTH, SHOT, HIMSELF

Idiom **Shoot yourself in the foot.**
Meaning **To say or do something that has a negative effect on yourself.**
Example **He shop himself in the foot by telling him the truth.**

Question: I told you not to say that to him. can't you remember?
Possible answer: Yes I know. I went and shot myself in the foot.

Word translations.

Stand Suporte Fancy Extravagante
Enough Suficiente Shoot Atirar
Decision Decisão Eldest Mais Velho
Special Especial Footloose Ser Livre
Dance Dança Free Livre
Best O melhor Wrong Errado
Forward Para a Frente Mistake Erro
Firm Firme Drive Dirigir
Loose Solto Show Mostrar
Alone Sozinho Shoe Sapato

Please note that some translations are not literal. They are as close to the meaning of the idiom and word as is possible.

Teaching Point

Practice the new words by repeating them over and over and ask the student to repeat the idioms by using the Tagging principle to prompt the student and then repeat together by using the Tandeming technique until the student can recite independently.

Foot & Finger Idioms (3)

451).

FOOTHOLD, ESTABLISH, MARKET, BUSINESS

Idiom **Get a foothold**
Meaning **Means to establish yourself in something or at somewhere.**
Example **We need to get a foothold in the phone market while there is money to be made.**

Question: My brother has started a new business selling coal to Newcastle. Do you think its a good idea.
Possible answer: No absolutely not. He will never get a foothold in that kind of business. Its stupid.

452).

MOUTH, REALLY, REACTED, FUTURE

Idiom **Put your foot in your mouth**
Meaning **To say something that you shouldn't have said.**
Example **I really put my foot in my mouth and now he wont talk to me.**

Question: I knew I´d put my foot in my mouth when she reacted in the way she did.
Possible answer: You must try and think before you open your mouth in the future.

453).

DIG, HEELS, STUBBORN, CHANGE, MIND

Idiom **To dig your heels in**
Meaning **Not to change your mind.**
Example **I am going to dig my heels in. She wont be going out this weekend.**

Question: Do you change your mind a lot?
Possible answer: Most of the time I dig my heels in and I stubborn.

454).

DISCOUNT, STEAL, CAUGHT, SHOP LIFTING, HONEST

Idiom **Five finger discount**
Meaning **To steal something from a shop.**
Example **He was caught shop lifting this morning.**

Question: Have you ever used the five finger discount method of shopping?
Possible answer: No of course not. I'm an honest person.

455).

BURNT, TRANSACTION, BOUGHT, FINGERS, WATCH

Idiom **Get your fingers burnt**
Meaning **To make a bad transaction. Buy something that's not worth the money you paid.**
Example **I bought that car last year and really got my fingers burnt.**

Question: Have you ever had your fingers burnt?
Possible answer: Yes, I bought a really bad watch on Ebay.

456).

ONCE, WAITING, START, TELLING

Idiom **Get your finger out.**
Meaning **To start work now. At once.**
Example **Come on get your finger out, I'm waiting.**

Question: If I told you to get your finger out what would I mean?
Possible answer: You would be telling me to begin now. At once.

457)

HANGING, FINGERNAILS, ARRIVED, CHECKED, PAYDAY

Idiom **Hanging on by the fingernails.**
Meaning **Just about staying somewhere or doing something.**
Example **I was just hanging on by my fingernails when you arrived and saved me.**

Question: I was just about hanging on by my fingernails when my next pay check arrived.
Possible answer: Next time tell me and I will lend you some money until payday.

458).

CROSSED, DRIVING, TEST, WINNING

Idiom **Keep your fingers crossed**
Meaning **To hope for something to happen.**
Example **I'm keeping my fingers crossed for you tomorrow. Good luck with your driving test.**

Question: I could do with winning some money on the lottery, I really need some cash. Do you think I could win?
Possible answer: Well keep your fingers crossed and maybe it will happen.

459).

LIFT, SHOPPING, MANAGE, BECAUSE, MYSELF, YOURSELF, CARRIED

Idiom **Don't lift a finger.**
Meaning **Not doing any work.**
Example **He didn't lift a finger to help me. I carried the shopping home all by myself.**

Question: Why didn't you lift a finger to help me this morning?
Possible answer: Because I though you could manage by yourself.

460).

REMEMBER, SITUATION, GARAGE, KNOW, GUY

Idiom **Can't put my finger on it.**
Meaning **Can't think or remember a situation.**
Example **I know you from somewhere but can't put my finger on it.**

Question: I know him from somewhere but I can't put my finger on it. Who is he?
Possible answer: That's the guy from the garage down the road.

Word translations.

Foothold Ponte de Apoio Honest Honesto
Establish Estabelecer Once Uma vez
Market Mercado Hang Caimento
Mouth Boca Fingernail Unha
React Reagir Cross Aravessar
Dig Escavação Test Teste
Change Alterar Carry Transportar
Heel Calcanhar Remember Lembrar
Discount Desconto Situation Situação
Steal Roubar Lift Levantar

Please note that some of the translations are not literal. They are as close to the meaning of the idiom or actual word as is possible.

End of lesson Twenty-three (Forty minutes)

It's important at this point to review all of the words and idioms one more time before moving onto lesson number twenty four. the student is comfortable then it's safe to move forward.

End of lesson test

Below you will find a short test which covers the twenty-third lesson of idioms. This short twenty minute test is meant as a revision and not as a marker for how well the student is progressing. Tests all the way through these books are for motivational and revision purposes only. People perform differently under exam pressures and we believe that a student's primary aim is to learn a new skill and not to prove his or her worth.

So, when giving the tests keep it light.

The tests consist of ten questions and a short dictation containing some of the words introduced.

You will also find the answering sheets and answer sheets below. Please feel free to print off as many as needed for each student.

End of lesson twenty three dictation

My son is old enough to stand on his own two feet now, he was twenty last week. At his birthday party everyone was dancing but it was clear that he has two left feet. His dancing was ridiculous. I know he was trying to put his best foot forward and impress his friends but he just looked silly on the dance floor. I told him to stop and sit down but he just dug his heels in and continued. His girlfriend lost her bag with all her money and things in it. Clearly someone had performed a five finger discount on her. She was very upset.

Ten questions about idioms.
Enter the missing words in the right hand column.

1 Learn to ______ on your own two feet.
2 I have ______ left ______.
3 To put your _____ foot forward.
4 I put my ______ in it.
5 He didn't put a foot ______.
6 I shot ______ in the foot.
7 I really put my foot in my _____.
8 He dug his ______ in.
9 He stole something from the supermarket using the _____ finger _____ method.
10 We are running out of time we need to ____ our fingers _____.

Review the answers on the following page

Once the test is completed do a full review of all the errors and questions the student may have.

It's important to note that each book carries the same introduction and instruction as the first book. This is so that any stage of instruction can be bought if your student has a higher level of English than a complete beginner. You can buy a stage four book and still learn about the method of teaching without buying the whole series.

Test Answers

1	Stand
2	Two, Feet
3	Best
4	Foot
5	Wrong
6	Myself
7	Mouth
8	Heels
9	Five, Discount
10	Get, Out

Lesson Twenty Four

Finger and Leg Idioms (4)

461).

HANDS,THUMBS, DELICATE, LACES, NEEDLES, ABLE, SHOE

Idiom All fingers and thumbs.
Meaning Not able to do something delicate with your hands.
Example Can you help me to tie my shoe laces please. I'm all fingers and thumbs?

Question: Can you help me to thread a needle please?
Possible answer: Why? Are you all fingers and thumbs?

462)

SEA, SHIP, BOAT, FOUND, TRIP, ACROSS

Idiom Sea legs.
Meaning Means to feel OK on a ship or boat.
Example I soon found my sea legs during the trip across to the island.

Question: Are you OK travelling on boats and ships.
Possible answer: Yes, my sea legs are pretty good. I don't usually feel seasick.

463).

SLIP, OPPORTUNITY, LOSE, BOUGHT, THROUGH, WAITED

Idiom **Let slip through your fingers**
Meaning **To lose an opportunity.**
Example **I was going to buy that car because it was a bargain, but I waited to long and it slipped through my fingers.**

Question: I really wanted that old bike but it just slipped through my fingers.
Possible answer: You should have been quicker and bought it last week.

464).

BONE, TIRED, THOUGHT, WORKING

Idiom **Work your fingers to the bone**
Meaning **To work very, very hard.**
Example **I have been working my fingers to the bone. I'm so tired.**

Question: I have worked my fingers to the bone this weekend. I thought you might have helped me.
Possible answer: You should have asked me. I would have helped.

465).

RAP, KNUCKLES, WARNING, LATE, EARLY

Idiom **A rap on the knuckles.**
Meaning **To be given a warning. To told off.**
Example **He gave me a rap on the knuckles for being late this morning.**

Question: Did you give him a rap on the knuckles for being late again?
Possible answer: Yes, he was late just too many times.

466).

STICKING, SORE, CONSPICUOUS, MATCH, WEARING

Idiom **Sticking out like a sore thumb.**
Meaning **To be very conspicuous.**
Example **Its not a good to go to the football match wearing the oppositions shirt.**

Question: Who did that to you. You have a black eye.
Possible answer: I was in a pub last night and got into a fight. I know my eye sticks out like a sore thumb.

467).

UNDER, CONTROLLED, PARTNER, GIRLFRIEND, CRAZY

Idiom **Under your thumb.**
Meaning **To be controlled by your partner.**
Example **My last girlfriend had me under her thumb.**

Question: What was your last girlfriend like?
Possible answer: She drove me crazy. I was really under her thumb.

468).

CLOSE, TROUBLE, TOOLS

Idiom **On hand**
Meaning **To have something or someone close by.**
Example **If I get into trouble my mother is on hand to help.**

Question: Where are you tools?
Possible answer: They are here. I have them at hand.

469).

GLOVE, TOGETHER, BREAKING, ACCORDING, ARRESTED

Idiom **Hand in glove**
Meaning **To work to together with someone. Two things that go together.**
Example **The two boys worked hand in glove when breaking into the shop.**

Question: Do you know who broke into the garage last night?
Possible answer: Yes, according to the police, two guys from the next town were working hand in glove. But the police have arrested them.

470).

JOB, TOGETHER, NEXT, FINISHED, QUICKER

Idiom **Hand in hand.**
Meaning **To do something together.**
Example **They did the long walk hand in hand.**

Question: We are working hand in hand with the garage in the next street to get this job finished.
Possible answer: You will finish the job much quicker doing that.

Word table with translations.

Thumb	Polegar	Through	Através
Delicate	Delicado	Quick	Rápido
Laces	cadarço	Bought	Comprou
Sea	Mar	Bone	Osso
Boat	Barco	Tired	Cansado
Ship	Navio	Rap / Hit	Bater
Island	Ilha	Knuckles	Junta
Travel	Viagem	Sore	Dolorido
Opportunity	Oportunidade	Sticking	Degola
Slip	Escorregar	Match	Jogo

Please note that some of the translations are not literal. They are as close to the meaning of the idiom or the actual word as is possible.

Teaching Point

Practice the new words by repeating them over and over and ask the student to repeat the idiom by using the Tagging principle to prompt the student and then repeat together by using the Tandeming technique until the student can recite independently.

Finger & Leg Idioms (5)

471).

GIG, GUITAR, ADMIT, CONGRATULATIONS, PERFORMANCE

Idiom **Got to hand it to you.**
Meaning **Got to admit to are right. Or congratulations.**
Example **I have to hand it to you, the performance was great.**

Question: Were you impressed with my performance last night at the gig?
Possible answer: Yes, I have got to hand it to you, your guitar playing has certainly improved.

472).

HANDED, PLATE, WORKING, BUSINESS, FAMILY

Idiom **Handed on a plate.**
Meaning **To be given something without working for it.**
Example **He was handed his fathers business on a plate.**

Question: Do you know how he got all of his money.
Possible answer: As I understand it he was handed it all on a plate from his family. He didn't earn a penny of it.

473).

BITE, ACCEPT. QUICKLY, CHEAP, BARGAIN, OFFERED

Idiom **Bite your hand off.**
Meaning **To accept something from someone very quickly.**
Example **The car is cheap. I'm going to bite his hand off.**

Question: He offered me his car for less than it was worth. What should I do?
Possible answer: Its a bargain. You should bite his hand off.

474).

FORCE, DECISION, DIFFICULT, LONGER

Idiom **Force someone's hand**
Meaning **To make someone do something or make someone make a decision quicker.**
Example **I had to force his hand. It was getting more and more difficult to wait.**
Question: I have been waiting for him to make a decision but I can't wait much longer. What should I do?
Possible answer: You are going to have to do something to force his hand and make him make a decision soon.

475).

FREE, ANYTHING, PAINT, PORTRAIT, SUGGEST, HAPPENS

Idiom **A free hand.**
Meaning **Free to do anything you want.**
Example **I was given a free hand on how to paint his portrait.**

Question: I have asked him to paint a portrait of me. What style do you suggest I get him to paint?
Possible answer: Just give him a free hand and see what happens.

476).

PARTY, CALL, SPENDING, BEFORE

Idiom **Get out of hand.**
Meaning **The party got out of hand and he had to call the police.**
Example **Don't let her spending get out of hand.**

Question: I'm going to ask the family living next door to turn the music down a little. They are having a party.
Possible answer: I would ask them to calm down before it gets out of hand and we have to call the police.

477).

HEAVY, STRONGLY, LITTLE, HANDED, POLITE, RULES

Idiom **Heavy handed.**
Meaning **To do something strongly.**
Example **He was a little heavy handed with his your son.**

Question: Do you think I was a little heavy handed with my son this morning?
Possible answer: No not really because he has to learn the rules of how to be polite to people.

478).

DOING, LACK, ORGANISATION, CLEAR

Idiom **Left hand doesn't know what the right is doing.**
Meaning **Someone who doesn't know what he is doing. A lack of organisation.**
Example **He was so confused that his right hand didn't know what his left was doing.**

Question: I don't think he knows what he is doing. Do you?
Possible answer: No, its clear his left hand doesn't know what his right is doing.

479).

LIVE, MOUTH, POOR, PERIOD

Idiom **Live from hand to mouth.**
Meaning **To live on very little money. If any! A very poor period of time in your life.**
Example **He was living hand to mouth until he got a job.**

Question: I have just been through a very tough period. But I now have a new job.
Possible answer: Its not fun living hand to mouth.

480).

HAIR, NOTHING

Idiom **A bad hair day.**
Meaning **A bad day. Nothing going right today.**
Example **He is having a bad hair day today.**

Question: Yesterday was a bad day. Nothing went to plan.
Possible answer: Did you have a bad hair day?

End of lesson twenty four (Forty minutes)

Teaching Point

It's important at this point to review all of the words and idioms one more time before moving onto section nine. Once the student is comfortable then it's safe to move forward.

Word translations.

Admit Admitir Hair Cabelo
Congratulations Parabéns Nothing Nada
Performance Atuação Portrait Retrato
Plate Prato Suggest Sugerir
Business Negócio Spend Passar
Bite Morder Heavy Pesado
Accept Aceitar Organisation Orgaização
Bargain Barganha Confused Confuso
Force Força Period Periodo
Decision Decisão Right Direito/ Correto

Please note that some of the translations are not literal. They are as close to the meaning of the idiom or actual word as is possible.

End of lesson twenty four test

Below you will find a short test which covers the twenty-fourth and final lesson of this book. This short twenty minute test is meant as a revision and not as a marker for how well the student is progressing.

Tests all the way through these books are for motivational and revision purposes only. People perform differently under exam pressures and we believe that a student's primary aim is to learn a new skill and not to prove his or her worth. So, when giving the tests keep it light. The tests consist of ten yes or no questions and a short dictation containing some of the words introduced.

You will also find the answering sheets below. Please feel free to print off as many as needed for each student.

End of section dictation.

We set off on our trip and I soon found my sea legs. As we boarded the ship carrying our bags I felt all fingers and thumbs. The ships crew soon offered to help but I told them not to be too heavy handed with my delicate equipment. I have got to hand it to them though, they did a very good job of everything. When they offered I had to bite their hands off because the bags were so heavy. Once on board the crew gave us a free hand to go anywhere and do anything we wanted to. The first morning after a very rough night it was clear that my wife was having a bad hair day. She was in a very bad mood all day.

Ten questions about idioms.
Enter the missing words in the right hand column.

1 I was all ______ and thumbs this morning.
2 The crossing was rough but we soon got our ____ legs.
3 I let the car slip through my ______.
4 We are now working _____ in glove.
5 I have got to _____ it to ______.
6 His fortune was ______ to him on a plate.
7 I bit his _____ off. The car was a bargain.
8 I gave him a _____ hand when paining my portrait.
9 I thought the bouncer was a little _____ handed.
10 I'm having a _____ hair _____.

Review the answers on the following page

Once the test is completed do a full review of all the errors and questions the student may have.

Notes

Test answers

1	Finger
2	Sea
3	Fingers
4	Hand
5	Had, You
6	Handed
7	Hand
8	Free
9	Heavy
10	Bad, Day

Lesson Twenty Five

Clock Idioms (1)

481).

AGAINST, SHORT, RACE, FINISHED

Idiom **Against the clock**
Meaning **Means to do something in a short time.**
Example **We are racing against the clock to get this job finished.**

Question: Have you ever run in a race against the clock?
Possible answer: Yes, I ran in a ten kilometre race last week. I came twenty third.

482).

NEVER, BETTER, ARRIVING, STILL, SUPPOSE

Idiom **Better late than never.**
Meaning **To arrive late is better than not arriving at all.**
Example **Its ten past nine. You are late again. Still, I suppose its better late than never.**

Question: How often do you arrive late for your class?
Possible answer: All the time as you know.

483).

COCK, RECORD, CLOCKED, OFFICE, FACTORY

Idiom **Clock in.**
Meaning **To record the time you arrived at work.**
Example **I clocked in at eight am this morning. Just on time.**

Question: Do you have to clock in at work?
Possible answer: No, I work in an office. But the people in the factory have to.

484).

LEAVE

Idiom **Clock out.**
Meaning **To record the time you leave work at night.**
Example **I have to clock in and out every day.**

Question: What time did you clock out last night?
Possible answer: I think it was about 6.10pm

485).

CUT, JUST, SPARE, NEARLY, MISSED, BUS STOP.

Idiom **To cut things short.**
Meaning **To arrive only just on time. With no time to spare.**
Example **You cut it a little short this morning. You nearly missed the bus.**

Question: Do you ever cut it short catching the bus in the morning?
Possible answer: Every morning. I have to run to the bus stop.

486).

DONKEY, TEACHING

Idiom **Donkey´s years.**
Meaning **For a very long time.**
Example **I've been working here for donkey´s years.**

Question: How long have you been teaching Spanish?
Possible answer: A long time, donkey´s years.

487).

WIRE, DOWN

Idiom **Down to the wire.**
Meaning **To not allow much time to finish or arrive.**
Example **It was down to the wire if the job was going to be finished or not. But we made it on time.**

Question: Did you arrive for your exam on time this morning?
Possible answer: Only just. It was down to the wire again.

488).

ELEVENTH, MOMENT, COMPLETED, LEAVE

Idiom **At the eleventh hour.**
Meaning **Just did it on time. To do something at the last moment.**
Example **He completed it at the eleventh hour.**

Question: Do you ever do anything at the eleventh hour?
Possible answer: I never leave myself enough time to do anything in life!

489).

LONG, FUTURE, USEFUL, INTEND, LEARNING

Idiom **In the long run.**
Meaning **To look to the future.**
Example **In the long run I think it will be useful.**

Question: Do you think learning Chinese is going to be any use to you?
Possible answer: Well, in the long run yes. I intend to go there one day.

490).

AROUND, CORNER, BIRTHDAY, BUY, MAYBE

Idiom **Just around the corner**
Meaning **Very soon.**
Example **My birthday is just around the corner. What are you going to buy me?**

Question: Our holiday is just around the corner. I think maybe in two or three weeks. Do you know where I am going?
Possible answer: No, where are you going.

Word translations.

Against Contra Factory Fábrica
Finish Fim, Acabamento Spare Livre / Extra
Race Corrida Nearly Quase
Never Nunca Donkey Burro
Better Melhor Wire Arame
Arrive Chegar Moment Momento
Suppose Supor Leave Deixar
Clock (verb) Cronometrar Intend Pretenter
Record Registro / Gravar Useful Util
Office Escritório FutureFuturo

Please note that some of the translations are not literal. They are as close to the meaning of the idiom or word as is possible.

Teaching Point

Practice the new words by repeating them over and over and ask the student to repeat the idiom by using the Tagging principle to prompt the student and then repeat together by using the Tandeming technique until the student can recite independently.

Time Idioms (2)

491).

MOMENT, TRUTH, ANNOUNCED, RESULT, WONDER

Idiom **The moment of truth**
Meaning **The time the truth or result is announced.**
Example **The moment of truth has arrived. I wonder who won.**

Question: If I said, the moment of truth has arrived with your studies. What would I mean?

Possible answer: Maybe its time to do my end of stage exam.

492).

NEVER, MONTH, DRIVING, CHANCE

Idiom **Never in a month of Sundays.**
Meaning **Something will never happen.**
Example **He will never pass his driving test in a month of Sundays.**

Question: Do you think I'm ready to pass my exam?
Possible answer: Not a chance. Not in a month of Sundays. I suggest you study for a few more weeks.

493).

REPEATEDLY, LESSON

Idiom **Time after time.**
Meaning **To do something repeatedly. Over and over again.**
Example **I have told him time and time again to be here on time.**

Question: Do I have to tell you to arrive on time in the morning for your lesson?
Possible answer: Yes, you have told me time after time.

494).

RETIRED

Idiom **To have time on your hands.**
Meaning **To have a lot of time to do nothing.**
Example **I have a lot of time on my hands now I'm retired.**

Question: Are you busy at the moment?
Possible answer: No, I have a lot of time on my hands.

495).

FLIES, REMEMBER, PARTICULARLY

Idiom **Time flies**
Meaning **Time goes very fast.**
Example **How time flies. I can remember you when you were young.**

Question: Do you think that time flies?
Possible answer: Yes, particularly as you get older.

496).

DISCO, CONCERTS, GREAT, WILD

Idiom **Time of your lives (life).**
Meaning **To have fun.**
Example **We were having the time of our lives.**

Question: When you were young, did you have a great time?
Possible answer: Yes, we had the time of our lives. Discos, concerts, motorcycles etc. It was wild.

497).

SIDE, PARTICULAR, WORLD, MAYBE

Idiom **Have time on your side.**
Meaning **To have a lot of time. In particular when you are young.**
Example **He is only young. He has time on his side.**

Question: When are you going to travel around the world?
Possible answer: Maybe in a few years. I have a lot of time on my side.

498).

RIPE, CONDITIONS

Idiom **Time is ripe.**
Meaning **Means its the right time to do it. "NOW"**
Example **Lets do it now while the time and conditions are right.**

Question: When are you going to travel?
Possible answer: I'm thinking of going now while the time is ripe.

499).

TICKING, RUNNING, QUICKLY

Idiom **Time is ticking.**
Meaning **Time is running out quickly.**
Example **Come on time is ticking lets go.**

Question: I'm getting older, do you know?
Possible answer: Yes I know. How old are you tomorrow?

500).

BUY, ANOTHER, MOVE, SAVE

Idiom **For the time being.**
Meaning **To do now.**
Example **For the time being lets stay in the house and buy another next year.**

Question: Do you mind if we don't move houses for the time being.
Possible answer: No of course not. We can save a little more money.

Word translations

Moment Momento Wild Selvagem
Announce Anunciar Side Lado
Wonder Maravilha Ripe Madura
Chance Chance / Oportunidade Conditions Condiçãos
Never Nunca Ticking Tique-taque
Repeatedly Repetidamente Quickly Rapidamente
Retire Aposentar Save Salvar
Flies Moscas Buy Comprar
Particularly Particularmente
Concert Concerto

Please note that some of the translations are not literal. They are as close too the meaning of the idiom or word as is possible.

End of lesson twenty five (Forty minutes)

It's important at this point to review all of the words and idioms one more time before moving onto lesson number twenty three. Once the student is comfortable, then it's safe to move forward.

End of lesson Twenty-five test

Below you will find a short test which covers the lesson above. This short twenty minute test is meant as a revision and not as a marker for how well the student is progressing.

Tests all the way through these books are for motivational and revision purposes only. People perform differently under exam pressures and we believe that a student's primary aim is to learn a new skill and not to prove his or her worth. So, when giving the tests keep it light. The tests consist of ten simple questions and a short dictation containing some of the words introduced.

You will also find the answering sheets and answer sheets below. Please feel free to print off as many as needed for each of your students.

End of lesson twenty-five dictation

So the moment of truth has arrived, she said. I replied, yes, time flies. I said to my mother this morning that time was ticking and we really should start our trip. I reminded her that once we leave we would have the time of our lives and it would be great fun. Really, we should leave now whilst we have time on our side. She replied that for the time being she was happy to just wait a few more months and wait until the time is ripe.

Ten questions about idioms.
Enter the missing words in the right hand column.

1 So, the moment of ______ has finally arrived.
2 I wont ever do that. Never on a _______.
3 I have told that boy time after _____ not to rise his bike on my garden.
4 You know I think I'm getting older. How _____ flies.
5 They were having the ______ of their _____.
6 They have time on the ______.
7 Lets go now while the ______ is ______.
8 Time is ______ in everyone's lives.
9 Lets stay here for the time ______.
10 He will be OK in the ______ run.

Review the answers on the following page

Once the test is completed do a full review of all the errors and questions the student may have.

Notes

Test Answers

1	Truth
2	Sundays
3	Time
4	Time
5	Time, Lives
6	Side
7	Time, Ripe
8	Ticking
9	Being
10	Run

Lesson Twenty Six

Each section in this e-book contains twenty English idioms with meaning and examples. The student repeats the idiom until the pronunciation is correct and the meaning is understood. Where possible the Portuguese equivalent is compared alongside. Each e-book contains sixty idioms and a short self-test at the end.

Time Idioms (3)

501).

BORROWED, GRANDMOTHER, ILL, LIVING

Idiom **Living on borrowed time.**
Meaning **Should be dead now .**
Example **He is very ill. He is living on borrowed time.**

Question: How is your grandmother?
Possible answer: She is very ill. The doctor said that she's living on borrowed time.

502).

LOSE, TRACK, NOTICE

Idiom **Lose track of time.**
Meaning **Not noticing the time.**
Example **Its late, I lost track of the time. I had better go home.**

Question: Do you know what the time it is?
Possible answer: Yes, its 6pm. I lost track of the time.

503).

MATTER, EVENTUALLY, HAPPEN, POSITIVE

Idiom **Only a matter of time.**
Meaning **Something will happen eventually.**
Example **Its only a matter of time until I win the lottery.**

Question: When do you think you will win the lottery?
Possible answer: I'm staying positive. Its only a matter of time.

504).

HATE, LATE, NICK OF TIME, FINISHED

Idiom **In a nick of time.**
Meaning **Arrived or finished with no time to spare.**
Example **I arrived at work in a nick of time, I hate being late.**

Question: What time did you arrive for your lesson?
Possible answer: I arrived at one minute to six. Just in a nick of time. I hate being late.

505).

PRESSED, ENOUGH, LONGER

Idiom **Pressed for time.**
Meaning **Don't have enough time.**
Example **Sorry I can't help you right now, I'm pressed for time. maybe later.**

Question: Do you have time to stay a little longer?
Possible answer: No, I'm sorry I can't. I am a little pressed for time today.

506).

FINISH, CUSTOMER, AGAINST

Idiom **A race against time.**
Meaning **Not enough time to finish.**
Example **We must get a move on. Its a race against time We must finish this customer order by 5pm**

Question: Do you ever have to race against time?
Possible answer: Yes, every morning. I'm always late for the bus.

507).

STAND, MOVIE, STOOD, TEST

Idiom **Stand the test of time.**
Meaning **Will last for a long time.**
Example **This movie certainly has stood the test of time.**

Question: Do you like old movies?
Possible answer: Yes, I love them, some really do stand the test of time.

508).

SHIP, SAILED, AVAILABLE, ANYMORE

Idiom **Your ship has sailed**
Meaning **A missed opportunity.**
Example **Is the offer still open? No, sorry your ship has sailed.**

Question: If I said that your that ship has sailed. What would I mean?
Possible answer: You would be telling me that I had missed the opportunity and its not available anymore.

509).

NEEDED, SHELF, EXCEEDED, LENGTH

Idiom **Shelf life**
Meaning **The length of time something is available or good.**
Example **He has exceeded his shelf life.**
Question: If someone told you that your shelf life has expired, what would they mean?
Possible answer: They would mean that I'm no longer needed.

510).

SIGN, NATURE, NOWADAYS

Idiom **Sign of the time.**
Meaning **It the nature things, what life is like these days.**
Example **Everything is so expensive nowadays. Its a sign of the times.**

Question: Do you think food is getting too expensive?
Possible answer: Yes, but its a sign of the times. What can we do about it?

Word translations.

Borrow Emprestar Stood Ficou
Track Pisto / Seguir / Caminho Shelf Prateleira
Matter Assunto Exceed Exceder
Nick (small) Pequeno Length Comprimento
Pressed Presado Nowadays Hoje em dia
Enough Suficiente Nature Natureza
Finish Fim / Acabamento / Terminar Sign Sinal
Customer Cliente
Against Contra
Stand Suporte

Please note that some translations are not literal. They are as close to the meaning of the idiom and word as is possible.

Teaching Point

Practice the new words by repeating them over and over and ask the student to repeat the idioms by using the Tagging principle to prompt the student and then repeat together by using the Tandeming technique until the student can recite independently.

Time Idioms (cont.)

511).

BETWEEN, SHIFT WORK

Idiom **In the small hours**
Meaning **Early in the morning. Usually between 1am and 4 am**
Example **I didn't arrive home until the small hours.**

Question: Have you ever had to be at work in the small hours?
Possible answer: Yes, I sometimes do shift work and work between 10pm and 6am.

512).

HELL, FREEZE, DATE

Idiom **Until hell freezes over.**
Meaning **Never!**
Example **Hell will freeze over first before I go out with that girl again. She was crazy.**

Question: Would you have another date with that guy?
Possible answer: Hell will freeze over first!

513).

WARP, STUCK, DRESSING, OLD FASHIONED

Idiom **Stuck in a time warp.**
Meaning **Nothing has changed.**
Example **She dresses as though she is stuck in a time warp.**

Question: Do you like dressing in the latest fashions?
Possible answer: My mother says that the clothes I buy are so old fashioned. Like my taste is stuck in a time warp.

514).

IMMEMORIAL, EXISTED

Idiom **Since time immemorial**
Meaning **For ever. Existed for a very long time.**
Example **He has been coming her since time immemorial.**

Question: How long have you been studying Chinese?
Possible answer: Since time immemorial. Too long.

515).

EFFICIENTLY, ABLE, KNOWLEDGABLE, EMPLOYEE

Idiom **On the ball.**
Meaning **Able to something well. To be available now. Deal with something efficiently and now. Knowledgable.**
Example **Your new employee is really on the ball. He is very good at his job.**

Question: Are you good at your job?
Possible answer: Yes, I try to be on the ball and do my best.

516).

ACID, PROVE, EFFECTIVE, ULTIMATE

Idiom **Acid test.**
Meaning **To prove how effective something is.**
Example **I think your English course is very good. The acid test will be when I go to London.**

Question: Do you think you will be able to communicate when you get to London?
Possible answer: Well I have studied hard. But that will be the ultimate acid test.

517)

TRICK, SUCCEED, WHOLE, DIFFERENT

Idiom **Whole new bag of tricks.**
Meaning **To use everything you know to succeed in something new.**
Example **This process is a whole new bag of tricks.**

Question: I hear you have started studying Chinese. Is it different from studying English?
Possible answer: Of yes, its a whole new bag of tricks.

518).

CLOCKWORK, REGULAR

Idiom **Like clockwork.**
Meaning **To arrive or do something with regularity.**
Example **He arrives at 8.06am every day. Like clockwork.**

Question: What time do you have your dinner in the evenings?
Possible answer: My husband likes to eat at 8pm like clockwork.

519).

BULL, HORNS, SIMPLY

Idiom **Take the bull by the horns.**
Meaning **To deal with a problem with determination.**
Example **I took the bull by the horns and went to deal with him.**

Question: How do you begin studying for an exam?
Possible answer: I take the bull by the horns and simply study, study and study until I know what I am doing.

520).

DELIVER, IMPORTANT, EXPECTED

Idiom **Deliver the goods.**
Meaning **Do what is expected of you and on time.**
Example **He always delivers.**

Question: If I asked you to do something very important for me, could I rely on you?
Possible answer: Don't worry, I always deliver.

Word table with translations.

Between Entre Knowledge Coheciment
Shift work Trabalho por turnos Efficient Eficiente
Hell Inverno Acid Acido
Freeze Congelar Prove Provar
Warp Deformar Ultimate Final
Stuck Preso / Emperrado Trick Truque
Fashion Moda Succeed Suceder
Immemorial Imemorial Whole Todo
Exist Existir Clockwork Relógio
Able Capaz Horns Chifres / Buzina
Simply Simplesmente Expect Esperar
Deliver Entrgar

Please note that some of the translations are not literal. They are as close to the meaning of the idiom or actual word as is possible.

End of lesson Twenty- six (Forty minutes)

End of lesson test

Below you will find a short test which covers the twenty-third lesson of idioms. This short twenty minute test is meant as a revision and not as a marker for how well the student is progressing. Tests all the way through these books are for motivational and revision purposes only. People perform differently under exam pressures and we believe that a student's primary aim is to learn a new skill and not to prove his or her worth.

So, when giving the tests keep it light. The tests consist of ten questions and a short dictation containing some of the words introduced.

You will also find the answering sheets and answer sheets below. Please feel free to print off as many as needed for each student.

End of lesson twenty-six dictation

She arrived home in the small hours again. Her father said that she wont be going out again until hell freezes over as a punishment. Since time immemorial young people have been going out on Saturday nights. But nowadays its a whole new bag of tricks. Its quite dangerous. My dad says he always arrived home at midnight like clockwork on Saturday nights, but I don't really believe him. My dad also said that I needed to take the bull by the horns and improve my lifestyle.

Ten questions about idioms.
Enter the missing words in the right hand column.

1 I arrived home in the ______ hours.
2 He wont be going out again until hell _____ over.
3 Her dress sense is like she is stuck in a time_____.
4 ______ time in immemorial we have been going to Blackpool for our holiday.

5 He is always ______ the ball.
6 Going to London will be the _____ test.
7 This process is a ______ new bag of tricks.
8 He arrives _____ clockwork every morning.
9 I decided to take the bull by the ______.
10 He always ______ the goods.

Review the answers on the following page

Once the test is completed do a full review of all the errors and questions the student may have.

It's important to note that each book carries the same introduction and instruction as the first book. This is so that any stage of instruction can be bought if your student has a higher level of English than a complete beginner. You can buy a stage four book and still learn about the method of teaching without buying the whole series.

Test Answers

1	Small
2	Freezes
3	Warp
4	Since
5	On
6	Acid
7	Whole
8	Like
9	Horns
10	Delivers

Lesson Twenty Seven

Animal Idioms (4)

521).

BOSS, FISH, POND,

Idiom **A big fish in a small pond**
Meaning **An important person in a small place**
Example **He is a big fish in a very small pond.**

Question: What do you think of your new boss?
Possible answer: He seems like a big fish in a small pond working here.

522)

HORNET

Idiom **Mad as a hornet**
Meaning **Someone who is very angry.**
Example **My boss was as mad as a hornet this morning when I arrived late again.**

Question: Does your husband ever get angry?
Possible answer: Not usually, but this morning he really did hit the roof. He was as angry as a hornet.

523).

FLEA, WELCOME

Idiom A flea in your ear.
Meaning Something that is not welcome.
Example What do you think about your new manager? I has been a flea in our ears ever since he arrived.

Question: Am I a flea in your ear?
Possible answer: No of course not. We get on very well.

524).

ROOF, CALM, DEAR

Idiom Hit the roof.
Meaning To become very angry.
Example My dad hit the roof this morning. There wasn't any teabags.

Question: If I hit the roof with you, what would you say?
Possible answer: Simply, calm down dear.

525).

OYSTER

Idiom The world is your oyster.
Meaning You can have and get anything you want in life.
Example When you leave university the world will be your oyster.

Question: What will you do after you finish university?
Possible answer: I don't know yet. But the world is my oyster.

526).

BEE, FREE

Idiom As busy as a bee
Meaning To be very busy.
Example Are you free tomorrow? No, sorry. I'm as busy as a bee.

Question: Can you help me wash my car this afternoon please.
Possible answer: I'm sorry I can't. I am as busy as a bee.

527).

RED, LOBSTER, BURN, HAIR, BEACH

Idiom **As red as a lobster.**
Meaning **To be really sunburnt.**
Example **Do you cover your skin in the sun?**

Question: Do you burn easily in the sun?
Possible answer: Yes, I'm English and I have red hair. An hour on the beach and I look like a lobster

528).

SLIPPERY, EEL, DISHONEST

Idiom **As slippery as an eel**
Meaning **Undependable, Devious, can't be trusted.**
Example **That man is a slippery as an eel.**

Question: I don't trust that guy. Do you know him?
Possible answer: Yes, he is very dishonest. They say he is as slippery as an eel.

529).

TOAD

Idiom **A ugly as a toad.**
Meaning **Very ugly.**
Example **She really is as ugly as a toad.**

Question: Do you think I'm good looking?
Possible answer: Are you joking. A toad comes to mind!

530).

BIRDS, BEES, FACT, REPRODUCTION

Idiom **The birds and bees.**
Meaning **The facts about sex.**
Example **My mother told me about the birds and the bees when I was thirteen years old.**

Question: What does the idiom the birds and the bees mean?
Possible answer: Its all about life and sex and reproduction.

Word translations.

Boss Chefe Lobster Lagosta
Fish Peixe Burn Queimar
Pond Lago / Lagoa Beach Praia
Hornet Vespão Slippy Escorregadio
Roof Telhado Eel Enguia
Calm Calma Dishonest Desonesto
Dear Queido / Caro Toad Sapo
Oyster Ostra Fact fato
Busy Ocupa Reproduction Reprodução
Bee Ocupado Bird Passáro

Please note that some of the translations are not literal. They are as close to the meaning of the idiom or the actual word as is possible.

Teaching Point

Practice the new words by repeating them over and over and ask the student to repeat the idiom by using the Tagging principle to prompt the student and then repeat together by using the Tandeming technique until the student can recite independently.

Animal Idioms (cont.)

531).

BITTEN, BUG, EXCITED, TRAVELLING, HOBBIES, CARAVANNING

Idiom **Bitten by the bug**
Meaning **To become excited about something.**
Example **I was bitten by the bug and started travelling the world.**

Question: Do you have any hobbies.
Possible answer: Yes I was bitten by the caravanning bug some years ago.

532).

GILLS, SICK

Idiom **Blue around the gills**
Meaning **To look a little sick.**
Example **I sent him home today because he looked a little blue around the gills.**

Question: Do I look well today?
Possible answer: Not really. You look a little blue around the gills. You should go home and rest.

533).

BUG, ANNOY, INCREASE, FEES

Idiom **To bug someone**
Meaning **To annoy someone.**
Example **The problem has been bugging me all night.**

Question: Is anything bugging you at the moment?
Possible answer: Yes, you increased my school fees.

534).

CLAM, PERSONAL, QUESTIONS, DEPENDS

Idiom **To clam up.**
Meaning **To stop talking. To refuse to talk.**
Example **I was asking him some personal questions, then he just clammed up and would talk anymore.**

Question: If I asked you some personal questions will you clam up?
Possible answer: It depends on the questions.

535).

EMOTIONS, COLD, FISH, FRIENDLY

Idiom **A cold fish.**
Meaning **Someone who shows no emotions.**
Example **She is a cold fish. Don't bother asking her out.**

Question: Do you think I am friendly?
Possible answer: Sometimes you can be a cold fish.

536).

Idiom **Crocodile tears.**
Meaning **Not real tears.**
Example **No need to apologise they were only crocodile tears.**

Question: I thought she was really upset with me.
Possible answer: No, just crocodile tears. She was just pretending.

537).

KETTLE, ISSUE, ANOTHER

Idiom A different kettle of fish.
Meaning **A different issue or problem.**
Example **This is a different kettle of fish. I don't know the answer. You will have to ask someone else.**

Question: Can you teach me to speak Japanese too.
Possible answer: No only English. Japanese is another kettle of fish.

538).

GOTTEN, MESS

Idiom **A fine kettle of fish.**
Meaning **A mess, A problem.**
Example **This is a fine kettle of fish you have gotten me into.**

Question: Is everything OK at the moment?
Possible answer: No, my son has gotten me into a fine kettle of fish. I don't know what I'm going to do.

539).

FISHING, COMPLIMENTS, NICE

Idiom Fishing for compliments.
Meaning **Trying to get someone to say something nice about you.**
Example **She was only fishing for compliments.**

Question: Do you think I'm handsome dear?
Possible answer: You don't usually fish for compliments, are you ok?

540).

UNCOMFORTABLE

Idiom **A fish out of water.**
Meaning **To feel uncomfortable somewhere or with something.**
Example **When I arrived in Australia for the first time I felt like a fish out of water.**

Question: Are you comfortable living in Brazil?
Possible answer: Sometimes I feel like a fish out of water.

Word table with translations.

Bitten Mordido Emotions Emoção
Bug Aborrecer Kettle Chaleira
Caravanning Caravan ismo Issue Questão
Hobby Passatempo Gotten Começado
Travelling Viagens Mess Bagunça
Gills Guelras Fishing Pescaria
Annoy Aborrecer Compliment Elogio / Felicitar
Fees Honorários Uncomforfotable Desconfortável
Clam Catar / Molusco
Depend Depender

Please note that some of the translations are not literal. They are as close to the meaning of the idiom or actual word as is possible.

End of lesson twenty-seven test

Below you will find a short test which covers the twenty-fourth and final lesson of this book. This short twenty minute test is meant as a revision and not as a marker for how well the student is progressing.

Tests all the way through these books are for motivational and revision purposes only. People perform differently under exam pressures and we believe that a student's primary aim is to learn a new skill and not to prove his or her worth. So, when giving the tests keep it light. The tests consist of ten yes or no questions and a short dictation containing some of the words introduced.

You will also find the answering sheets below. Please feel free to print off as many as needed for each student.

End of section dictation.

My mother Told me about the birds and the bees when I was about thirteen years old. She started to get upset with me yesterday because she was fishing for compliments and I didn't respond the way she wanted. But they were only crocodile tears. Sometimes she can be a bit of a cold fish. I was bitten by the motorcycling bug after I went caravanning with friend last year. There was a guy on the campsite that had a Honda Goldwing, it was a stunning looking bike. I just had to get one.

Ten questions about idioms.
Enter the missing words in the right hand column.

1 When did you learn about the ____ and the ____?
2 I was bitten by the _____ last year.
3 She looked really quite sick. A little blue around the ______.
4 He was beginning to _____ me.
5 I was trying to get an explanation from him but then he just clammed ____.

6 That girl is a _____ fish. Don't bother with her.
7 Talk about _______ tears. She wasn't really upset at all.
8 Its a _______ kettle of fish now.
9 He was only ______ for compliments.
10 I felt like a _____ out of _____ for months.

Review the answers on the following page

Review the answers on the following page

Once the test is completed do a full review of all the errors and questions the student may have.

Test answers

1	Birds, Bees
2	Bug
3	Gills
4	Bug
5	Up
6	Cold
7	Crocodile
8	Different
9	Fishing
10	Fish, Water

Lesson Twenty Eight

Each lesson in this e-book contains twenty English idioms with explanations. As with the other e-books in this method the student repeats the idiom until the pronunciation is correct and the meaning is understood. Where possible the Portuguese equivalent is compared alongside. Each e-book contains sixty idioms and a short self-test at the end.

As this is the final section of this series it would be a good idea to do a complete revision simply by asking random questions about the previous idioms and questions.

Intelligence Idioms (1)

541).

UNDERSTAND, BEAT, BRAINS, IMPORTANT, COMPLICATED

Idiom	**To beat your brains out.**
Meaning	**To try very hard to understand something.**
Example	**Don't beat your brains out its not that important.**

Question: Did you understand what I was saying?
Possible answer: No, It was too complicated. Ok, well don't beat your brains out. Its not that important.

542).

DIRECT, FORGOTTEN

Idiom	**It beats me.**
Meaning	**I can't understand it.**
Example	**It beats me. What did he say?**

Question: What is direct speech?
Possible answer: It beats me. I have forgotten.

543).

BEYOND, IMPOSSIBLE, PHYSICS

Idiom **Its beyond me.**
Meaning **Impossible for me to understand.**
Example **Did you understand the meaning of what he tried to say? No, its beyond my understanding.**

Question: Do you understand physics?
Possible answer: No, even at school it was beyond me.

544).

ACCEPT, DISHONEST

Idiom **I wasn't born yesterday.**
Meaning **I don't accept things that seem to be dishonest.**
Example **Pull the other leg. I wasn't born yesterday.**

Question: What does pull the other leg mean?
Possible answer: It means don't try and tell me things that aren't true. I wasn't born yesterday you know?

545).

AWARE, WAKE UP

Idiom **To be on the ball.**
Meaning **To be aware of everything that is happening.**
Example **You have to be on the ball doing this job.**

Question: Are you on the ball first thing in the mornings?
Possible Answer: Not at all. It takes me three hours to wake up.

546).

TAIL, NOR, SPEECH, EXPLANATION

Idiom **Can't make head no tail of it.**
Meaning **Can't understand it at all.**
Example **Do you understand these instructions? No, I can't make head no tail of them.**

Question: Did I explain the difference between direct speech and indirect speech?
Possible answer: Yes, but I couldn't make head nor tail of your explanation.

547).

BLINDED, SCIENCE, CONFUSING

Idiom **Blinded by science.**
Meaning **Something very confusing.**
Example **He tried to explain but I was blinded by science.**

Question: What would I mean if I told you he blinded me with science?
Possible answer: You would mean that you didn't understand anything.

548).

BORN, TRUTH, ACCEPT, OF COURSE

Idiom **I wasn't born yesterday**
Meaning **Means that I am too experienced to accept just anything as truth. I will check it out first.**
Example **Don't tell me that. I wasn't born yesterday you know?**

Question: If I told you the sky was green, would you believe me?
Possible answer: Of course not, do you think I was born yesterday?

549).

CLUE, MULTIPLIED

Idiom **I don't have a clue**
Meaning **Means I don't know anything about it.**
Example **Do you know where David is, its 2am? I don't have a clue.**

Question: What's 5,000 multiplied by 4.34?
Possible answer: Beats me. I don't have a clue.

550).

GRIPS, FINALLY, COMPLICATED, STUDYING

Idiom **Come to grips with.**
Meaning **To start to understand something finally.**
Example **I have to get to grips with this new television, its a little complicated than the old one.**

Question: Did you get to grips with that new grammar I gave you to study?
Possible answer: Yes, finally after hours of studying it.

Word translations.

Understand Entender Accept Aceitar
Beat Não intendo Dishonest Deshonesto
Brains Miolos / Inteligência Awake Acordado / Desperto
Important Importante Tail Cauda
Complicated Complicado Nor Nem
Direct Direto Explanation Explicação
Forgotten Esquecido Blinded Cegado / Cego
Beyond Além Grips Agarrar com firmeza
Impossible Impossivel Multiply Multiplicar
Physics Fisica Clue Pista

Please note that some of the translations are not literal. They are as close to the meaning of the idiom or word as is possible.

Teaching Point

Practice the new words by repeating them over and over and ask the student to repeat the idiom by using the Tagging principle to prompt the student and then repeat together by using the Tandeming technique until the student can recite independently.

Indecision Idioms (1)

551).

COLLECT, CONTINUING, CLEARLY

Idiom	**Collect your thoughts.**
Meaning	**To think slowly and clearly**
Example	**I took a moment to collect my thoughts before I made my decision.**

Question: Do you ever make rushed decisions?
Possible answer: No, I prefer to take my time, collect my thoughts and then try to make a rational decision.

552).

SENSES, REALISE, ADVICE, CANCELLED

Idiom	**Come to your senses.**
Meaning	**To realise you were wrong.**
Example	**I'm glad you have finally come to your senses.**

Question: Are you still going to buy that old car?
Possible answer: No, after taking some advice, I finally came to my senses and cancelled my offer.

553).

KNOWLEDGE, COMMON, APPARENTLY

Idiom **Common knowledge.**
Meaning **Well known to everyone.**
Example **Its common knowledge that she is leaving.**

Question: Did you know that the guy living across the road is very ill?
Possible answer: Yes, apparently its common knowledge.

554).

PURPOSES, MISUNDERSTANDING, FREQUENTLY

Idiom **At cross purposes.**
Meaning **To have a misunderstanding with someone.**
Example **I'm at cross purposes with my girlfriend at the moment.**

Question: Do you always agree with people?
Possible answer: No, I am frequently at cross purposes with people at work.

555).

DUMBING, COMPLICATED

Idiom **Dumbing down.**
Meaning **Deliberately made less complicated to aid understanding.**
Example **We will have to dumb it down a little if we want people to really understand the physics.**

Question: Did you understand all the instructions?
Possible answer: Yes, some of it was quite complicated but for most it had been dumbed down a little.

556).

WIDE, CONSEQUENCES, ARRANGEMENT, ENROLL

Idiom Eyes wide open.
Meaning **To start something completely aware of the consequences.**
Example **I went into this arrangement with my eyes wide open.**

Question: When you enrolled in this school did you read the contract small print?
Possible answer: Yes I enrolled with my eyes wide open.

557).

MESSAGE

Idiom **Get the message.**
Meaning **To understand what was said to you.**
Example **I hope he got the message when he fell off his bike this morning.**

Question: Do you think he got the message this time?
Possible answer: Yes, I hope so. He needs to ride that bike much slower and carefully.

558).

PICTURE

Idiom **Get the picture**
Meaning **To finally understand something.**
Example **He finally got the picture after I told him to shut up.**

Question: I explained it to him a hundred times. Do you think he has go the picture now?
Possible answer: I hope so. It was crystal clear to me.

559).

MUD, UNDERSTANDABLE, CONFUSING, EXPLANATION, INSTRUCTIONS

Idiom **As clear as mud.**
Meaning **Not understandable at all. Very confusing.**
Example **His explanation was as clear as mud.**

Question: Did you read the instructions to your new TV?
Possible answer: I tried but they were in Chinese. As clear as mud!

560).

WISE, QUITE, QUICKLY

Idiom **Get wise to something.**
Meaning **To learn something that you weren't aware of before.**
Example **I got wise to him quite quickly.**

Question: Do you trust that guy?
Possible answer: At first I did, but I soon got wise to his lies.

Word translations.

Collect Coletar Frequently Freqüentemente
Continuing Continuar Dumbing Down Mais simples
Clearly Claramente Complicated Complicato
Senses Juizo Wide Grande
Advice Concelho Consequences Conseqüências
Cancelled Cancelado Arrangements Arranjos
Apparently Aparentemente Enrol Inscrever
Knowledge Conhecimento Picture Quadro
Purposes Propósito Mud Lama
Misunderstanding Mal-entendido Confusing Confuso

Please note that some of the translations are not literal. They are as close too the meaning of the idiom or word as is possible.

End of lesson twenty eight (Forty minutes)

End of lesson Twenty-eight test

Below you will find a short test which covers the lesson above. This short twenty minute test is meant as a revision and not as a marker for how well the student is progressing.

Tests all the way through these books are for motivational and revision purposes only. People perform differently under exam pressures and we believe that a student's primary aim is to learn a new skill and not to prove his or her worth. So, when giving the tests keep it light. The tests consist of ten simple questions and a short dictation containing some of the words introduced. You will also find the answering sheets and answer sheets below. Please feel free to print off as many as needed for each of your students.

End of lesson twenty-eight dictation

I hope she got the message about the problems we have here at the moment. I tried to get the message to her, but I think the true meaning of my message was dumbed down a little. We had been at cross purposes for a long time, but finally he saw sense and settled the argument. In the future we will be working with our eyes wide open to any potential problems. Lets take a moment to collect our thoughts before we make any more bad decisions.

Ten questions about idioms.
Enter the missing words in the right hand column.

1 Collect your _______________.
2 Come to your __________.
3 Its ________ knowledge.
4 At _______ purposes.
5 Dumbing ______.
6 _______ Wide _______.
7 Get the ________.
8 Get the _________.
9 As _________ as ______.
10 I got ______ to him.

Review the answers on the following page

Once the test is completed do a full review of all the errors and questions the student may have.

Test Answers

1	Thought
2	Senses
3	Common
4	Cross
5	Down
6	Eyes, Open
7	Message
8	Picture
9	Clear, Mud
10	Wise

Lesson Twenty Nine

Law & Order Idioms (1)

561).

BOARD

Idiom **Above board**
Meaning **Open an honest**
Example **I don't think the payment was completely above board.**

Question: When you paid the guy was it above board?
Possible answer: No, not really. I think he put the money in his back pocket.

562).

LAW, FELT, EVENTUALLY

Idiom **Long arm of the law.**
Meaning **The power given to the police.**
Example **He felt the long arm of the law eventually.**

Question: Have you ever been in trouble with the police?
Possible answer: No, I haven't, but my brother has felt the long arm of the law.

563).

BEHIND, CRIME

Idiom **Behind bars.**
Meaning **To be in prison**
Example **His friend has finally been put behind bars for what he did.**

Question: Have you ever been in prison?
Possible answer: I have visited a friend in prison, but I never been behind bars for a crime.

564).

DOUBT, GUILTY, MURDER

Idiom **Beyond reasonable doubt.**
Meaning **Without doubt. Something certain.**
Example **He was found guilty beyond any reasonable doubt of the murder.**

Question: Do you think he did the crime?
Possible answer: Yes, in my opinion, there is no doubt. He has guilt written all over his face.

565).

PROOF, CONFESSION, ISSUES

Idiom **Its black and white.**
Meaning **Its simple. Written proof of it.**
Example **I have his confession here in black and white.**

Question: Do you think this case is black and white?
Possible answer: No, I think there are other issues to consider.

566).

REPORT, WHISTLE, BLOW, AUTHORITIES, FIRED, HAPPENING

Idiom **Blow the whistle**
Meaning **To report something harmful to the authorities.**
Example **He blew the whistle and the manager as fired.**

Question: If you saw something dishonest happening in the street would you call the police.
Possible answer: It depends how serious it was. If it was hurting someone then I would blow the whistle on them.

567).

BRUSH, LAW, ENCOUNTER

Idiom A brush with the law.
Meaning **To come close to being in trouble with the police.**
Example **I had a brief encounter with the police this morning.**

Question: Have you ever had a brush with the law?
Possible answer: No, never. I'm a good girl.

568).

BREAKING AND ENTERING, FORCE, BUILDING, SENTENCED, THIEVES, BURGLED, LABOUR

Idiom **Breaking and entering.**
Meaning **Someone illegally entering a house or building by using force.**
Example **He was found guilty in court of breaking and entering and sentenced to six months hard labour.**

Question: Has your house ever been burgled?
Possible answer: Yes, it was last year while we were out shopping, but they caught the thieves and they were sentenced to two years behind bars.

569).

BURDEN, PROOF, ACCUSATION, DOUBT, PROVEN

Idiom **Burden of proof.**
Meaning **The law must prove that an accusation is true.**
Example **The burden of proof was just not there so the defendant was released.**

Question: What does the burden of proof mean?
Possible answer: It means that something has to be proven correct without any doubt.

570).

PORRIDGE, SPENDING, BARS, JAIL, HUSBAND

Idiom **Doing porridge**
Meaning **Spending time behind bars in prison.**
Example **My husband is doing porridge at the moment.**

Question: What's another word for jail or prison?
Possible answer: Porridge.

Word translations.

Board Mesa Bars Grades de uma prisão
Law Lei Jail Prisão
Felt Feltro Accusation Acusação
Crime Crime Authorities Autoridades
Doubt Dúvida Fired Despidido
Guilty Culpado Brush Escovar
Murder Assassinato Encounter Encontro
Proof Prova Thieves Ladrão
Confession Confissão Sentenced Condenado á Prisão
Porridge Tempo de prisão Burden Carga / Fardo

Please note that some translations are not literal. They are as close to the meaning of the idiom and word as is possible.

Teaching Point

Practice the new words by repeating them over and over and ask the student to repeat the idioms by using the Tagging principle to prompt the student and then repeat together by using the Tandeming technique until the student can recite independently.

Speed Idioms (1)

571).

STREAK, LIGHTNING, SPRINTER, JOGGER

Idiom **Like a streak of lightning.**
Meaning **Very, very fast.**
Example **The sprinter in the Olympic 100 meters final was like a streak of lightning.**

Question: Can you run fast?
Possible answer: No, I am only a jogger. But my brother runs very fast. He is like a streak of lightning, he is so fast.

572).

IMMEDIATELY, SICK

Idiom **At the drop of a hat.**
Meaning **To do something immediately.**
Example **I told him that, if he needs my help I would be there at the drop of a hat.**

Question: Would you be willing to help me in the school. I have a teacher who is sick at the moment.
Possible answer: Yes of course, just call me and I´ll be there at the drop of a hat.

573).

INK

Idiom **Before the ink is dry.**
Meaning **Very quickly after something has finished.**
Example **He was after my job even before the contract for my new job was dry.**

Question: What does before the ink was dry mean?
Possible answer: It means immediately after an event has finished.

574).

BLINK, INSTANTANEOUS, SHOOTING STAR

Idiom **In the blink of an eye**
Meaning **So fast it was instantaneous.**
Example **The shooting star was gone in the blink of an eye.**

Question: I feel like I am getting older.
Possible answer: Yes me too. Life seems to go in the blink of an eye.

575).

HURRY, SHOUTING

Idiom **Get a move on.**
Meaning **Asking someone to hurry.**
Example **Come on, get a move on. We are going to be late.**

Question: Do you get up early in the morning?
Possible answer: No, my husband is always shouting, get a move on to me.

576).

LEAPS AND BOUNDS, PROGRESSING

Idiom **In leaps and bounds.**
Meaning **Progressing quickly.**
Example **His English is coming on in leaps and bounds.**

Question: How are you progressing with your Chinese?
Possible answer: Well, I certainly am not coming on in leaps and bounds. Its very slow.

577)

SHAKE, TRAVEL

Idiom **In two shakes.**
Meaning **To be there or do something very quickly.**
Example **Come on we are late. Don't worry we will be there in two shakes.**

Question: Does it take long to travel to school.
Possible answer: No, I'm here in two shakes. Its only about half a mile from my hom

578).

GREASE, LIGHTNING, SING

Idiom **Like grease lightning.**
Meaning **Very, very fast.**
Example **He runs like grease lightning.**

Question: Can you name me a song from the 70s movie GREASE?
Possible answer: Yes, GREASE LIGHTENING. Didn't John Travolta sing it? Yes, he did along with Olivia Newton John.

579).

BAT, HELL, SWIM, MEATLOAF (An American rock band)

Idiom **Like a bat out of hell.**
Meaning **Very, very fast.**
Example **He swims like a bat out of hell.**

Question: Who sung the song, BAT OUT OF HELL?
Possible answer: I know this one too. It was MEATLOAF.

580).

SHOT

Idiom	**Like a shot.**
Meaning	**Very, very fast**
Example	**I will be there like a shot. Just call me.**

Question: How long does it take you to get home after the lesson?
Possible answer: Not long. I'm usually home like a shot.

Word translations.

Streak Faixa / Camada Sing cantar
Lightning Relámpago Bat Morcego
Jogger Corrida Shot Tiro / Chute
Sprinter Corrida
Sick Doente
Ink Tinta
Blink Piscar
Instantaneous Instantáneo
Shooting star Estrela Cadente
Shouting Gritaria
Shake Agitar / Tremar
Grease Graxa / Gordura

Please note that some of the translations are not literal. They are as close to the meaning of the idiom or actual word as is possible.

End of lesson Twenty- nine (Forty minutes)

End of lesson test

Below you will find a short test which covers the twenty-nine of idioms. This short twenty minute test is meant as a revision and not as a marker for how well the student is progressing.

Tests all the way through these books are for motivational and revision purposes only. People perform differently under exam pressures and we believe that a student's primary aim is to learn a new skill and not to prove his or her worth.

So, when giving the tests keep it light.

The tests consist of ten questions and a short dictation containing some of the words introduced.

You will also find the answering sheets and answer sheets below. Please feel free to print off as many as needed for each student.

End of lesson twenty-nine dictation

He asked me to come quickly because there was a serious problem, so I got on my motorbike and was there in the blink on an eye. My bike goes like grease lightening, so I was there in a shot. I love rock music and one of my favourite tracks is Bat Out Of Hell by Meatloaf. Its a great track to ride to. I have lots of biker friends who would help me at the drop of a hat if I asked them. All I would need to do is call one of them and they would all be there in two shakes.

Ten questions about idioms.
Enter the missing words in the right hand column.

1 Like a streak of _________.
2 At the ______ of a hat.
3 Even before the ______ was dry.
4 My dad said, come on get a ______ on.
5 My Chinese is coming on leaps and _______.
6 I will be with you in ______ shakes.
7 Like _______ lightening.
8 Like a ______ out of ______ he sang.
9 Ill be there like a _______.
10 Grease ________.

Review the answers on the following page

Once the test is completed do a full review of all the errors and questions the student may have.

Notes

Test Answers

1	Lightening
2	Drop
3	Ink
4	Move
5	Bounds
6	Two
7	Grease
8	Hell
9	Shot
10	Lightening

Lesson Thirty

Shopping Idioms (1)

581).

AROUND, PREFER, CHEAPER

Idiom	**To shop around**
Meaning	**To visit lots of shops before you buy.**
Example	**I prefer to shop around to get the best price.**

Question: Do you generally shop around?
Possible answer: Not really, I usually buy most things online, its cheaper.

582)

ADDICTED, SHOPAHOLIC, LOADED, AFFORD

Idiom	**She is a shopaholic**
Meaning	**Someone who goes shopping a lot. Addicted to shopping.**
Example	**My wife is a shopaholic. Her credit card is always loaded to its limit.**

Question: Most women like shopping, right?
Possible answer: Not me, I only shop online if I want anything and only when I can afford.

583).

SPREE, SPENT, FORTUNE

Idiom	**A shopping spree**
Meaning	**To go out and buy a lot.**
Example	**My wife goes on a shopping spree every Saturday.**

Question: What did you do yesterday.
Possible answer: I went out on a shopping spree with my two sisters. We spent a fortune.

584).

SHOP, DROPPED

Idiom **Shop till you drop.**
Meaning **Go shopping until you are so tired you can't stand up.**
Example **I hate Christmas don't you? No, I love shopping until I drop.**

Question: My legs are so tired today. My wife made me shop until we dropped yesterday. It was fun but very tiring.
Possible answer: What did you do yesterday? The same as you.

585).

THERAPY, TAG ALONG

Idiom **Shopping therapy**
Meaning **Some people think that if you go shopping it makes you feel better.**
Example **I need some shopping therapy.**

Question: I need some shopping therapy too. Do you want to tag along?
Possible answer: Yes, great. Just what I needed too.

586).

MEANS, ALONG, FUN

Idiom **To tag along.**
Meaning **Go along too.**
Example **Do you want to come too. Yes, I´ll tag along for the fun.**

Question: What does tag along mean?
Possible answer: It means to go too.

587).

SHOPLIFTING, PAYING, CAUGHT

Idiom Shoplifting
Meaning **To steal things form shops without paying.**
Example **I was caught shoplifting once.**

Question: When.
Possible answer: When I was a student. We had no money or food.

588).

TRYING THINGS ON,

Idiom **Going window shopping.**
Meaning **Shopping, but not buying anything. Just looking at things. Trying things on etc.**
Example **We went window shopping on Saturday afternoon.**

Question: Did you buy anything this morning?
Possible answer: No, I was just window shopping. I don't have any money until the end of the month.

589).

FORMS, SALE, POUNDS, CASH

Idiom **Set up shop.**
Meaning **To start a business.**
Example **I set up shop at the car boot sale this morning and made fifty pounds.**

Question: Lets set up shop outside the school and do some marketing.
Possible answer: OK, I´ll get the membership forms and a petty cash box and some business cards.

590).

MATTERS, CHILL

Idiom **To talk shop.**
Meaning **To talk about business matters.**
Example **He loves to talk shop at dinner.**

Question: Does your husband bring his work home?
Possible answer: Yes, he talks shop over dinner and I always tell him to chill.

Word translations.

Prefer Preferir Tag along Vir
Around Em torno de Fun Diversão
Addicted Viviado Chill Acalme-se
Shopaholic Viciada em compras Means Meios
Loaded Completo Shoplift Roupar
Afford Permitir / dar Caught Capturados
Spree Maratona de compras Forms Forma
Fortune Fortuna Pounds Libras
Spent Passar / Gasto Cash Dinheiro
Dropped Caiu / Cair

Please note that some of the translations are not literal. They are as close to the meaning of the idiom or the actual word as is possible.

Teaching Point

Practice the new words by repeating them over and over and ask the student to repeat the idiom by using the Tagging principle to prompt the student and then repeat together by using the Tandeming technique until the student can recite independently.

Safety Idioms (1)

591).

BATTEN, HATCHES, STORM, BOARD UP, HURRICANE

Idiom **Batten down the hatches.**
Meaning **Prepare for danger. Like an oncoming storm.**
Example **There is a cyclone coming. Better batten down the hatches.**

Question: When was the last really bad storm around here?
Possible answer: Last year, we had a hurricane. We had to board up all windows.

592).

THROW, CAUTION, CONSCIOUS, PANTS, SEAT

Idiom **Throw caution to the wind.**
Meaning **To stop worrying about the danger of something.**
Example **Lets throw caution to the wind and do it anyway.**

Question: Are you usually safety conscious?
Possible answer: No, I life by the seat of my pants.

593).

PANTS, SEAT, DANGER, THROWING, CAUTION

Idiom **To live by the seat of your pants.**
Meaning **To almost live on the wrong side of danger. Just keeping within the limits of safety**
Example **When I was young I used to live by the seat of my pants.**

Question: To you live a normal life?
Possible answer: No not at all. I spend my life by the seat of my pants and throwing caution to the wind. After all you only live once.

594).

SHAVE, DISASTER, KNOCKED, ACCIDENT, TOUCH

Idiom **A close shave**
Meaning **A disaster nearly happened.**
Example **A car nearly knocked me off my bike this morning coming to school. It was a close shave.**

Question: When was your last car accident?
Possible answer: I haven't had one yet. Touch wood. But I've had a few close shaves.

595).

DICE, DEATH, DRIVING, CAREFUL

Idiom **Dice with death**
Meaning **Doing something dangerous.**
Example **Passing on the inside while driving is dicing with death.**

Question: Are you a careful driver?
Possible answer: Well, my mother keeps telling me I dice with death.

596).

DICEY, TRICKY, POTENTIALLY, DANGEROUS, TRAPPED, TRUCKS

Idiom **A dicey situation.**
Meaning **A potentially dangerous situation.**
Example **I got myself into a dicey situation this morning.**

Question: Oh what?
Possible answer: I was trying to cross a busy road and I got trapped between two large trucks. Tricky!

597).

FRAUGHT, RISKS, CLIMBING, MOTORWAY, SPEED, LIMITS

Idiom **Fraught with danger.**
Meaning **Something that is full risks.**
Example **Climbing a mountain alone is fraught with danger.**

Question: Driving down the motorway (free-way) too fast is fraught with danger, don't you think?
Possible answer: Yes, I always keep to the speed limits.

598).

HAIR, BREADTH, AVOID, NARROW

Idiom **By a hairs breadth.**
Meaning **Only just avoid something. Just avoided danger.**
Example **I missed that car by a hairs breadth.**

Question: How wide is a hairs breadth?
Possible answer: Very, very narrow. You just avoided an accident.

599).

SKIN, TEETH, NARROWEST, MARGIN, ESCAPE

Idiom **By the skin of your teeth**
Meaning **By the smallest, narrowest of margins.**
Example **He escaped death by the skin of his teeth. So close that teeth don't have skin.**

Question: How wide is the skin on your teeth?
Possible answer: Teeth don't have skin, so very narrow.

600).

HANG, SITUATION, FELL, WELL, RESCUED

Idiom **Hang on for dear life.**
Meaning **In a dangerous situation just about avoiding death.**
Example **I was just about hanging on for dear life when help arrived.**

Question: Have you ever been in a very dangerous situation?
Possible answer: Yes, I remember when I was a child I fell down a well. I only escaped by the skin of my teeth. I had to hang on for dear life until I was rescued.

End of lesson thirty and the last lesson of this course. (Forty minutes)

Congratulations on finishing the course.

Final Teaching Point

It's important at this point to review all of the words and idioms one more time.

Word translations.

Batten Travar Knocked Batido
Hatches Escotilhas Disaster Desastre
Board (v) Abordar Dice Jogar os dadod
Hurricane Furação Dicey Perigoso
Throw Jogar Driving Condução / Conduzir
Caution Cautela / Cuidado Tricky Complicado
Conscious Consciente Potentially Potencialmente
Pants Calças Trapped Preso
Seat Assento Fraught Cheio / Carregado
Shave Barbear Risks Riscos

Please note that some of the translations are not literal. They are as close to the meaning of the idiom or actual word as is possible.

End of lesson thirty test

Below you will find a short test which covers the thirtieth and final lesson of these books. This short twenty minute test is meant as a revision and not as a marker for how well the student is progressing.

Tests all the way through these books are for motivational and revision purposes only. People perform differently under exam pressures and we believe that a student's primary aim is to learn a new skill and not to prove his or her worth. So, when giving the tests keep it light. The tests consist of ten yes or no questions and a short dictation containing some of the words introduced.

You will also find the answering sheets below. Please feel free to print off as many as needed for each student.

End of section dictation.

There is a serious storm coming, we must batten down the hatches to make sure everything is safe. I don't like dicing with death when there is a huge storm coming. The last time we had a bad storm we only escaped by the skin of our teeth, because it was a dicey situation and getting worse by the hour. Storms, especially hurricanes are fraught with danger unless you take the proper precautions. There is no use living by the seat of your pants. I remember last December, we had a very close shave with a very dangerous storm.

Ten questions about idioms.
Enter the missing words in the right hand column.

1 Batten down the ________.
2 Throw _______ to the ________
3 Living by the seat of your _________.
4 It was a very ______ shave.
5 _______ with death.
6 A _______ situation.
7 Fraught with _______
8 I missed it by a _______ breadth
9 By the ______ of your ______
10 _______ on for dear life.

Review the answers on the following page

Once the test is completed do a full review of all the errors and questions the student may have.

Test answers

1	Hatches
2	Caution
3	Pants
4	Close
5	Dice
6	Dicey
7	Danger
8	Hairs
9	Teeth
10	Hang

Thank you for using our system of teaching and learning English.

Final Words

So, thank you for working through my book of idioms and fixed expressions. I hope you found it useful if not somewhat entertaining. The English language is só wonderful compared to other languages around the world. In my opinion of course. Having spent a lot of time traveling and now living and working in Brazil I have realised that the complexity of the English language is really second to none. The colour and diversity is truely outstanding, which is why I suppose it is the most popular language to date.

If you wish to take your studies a little futher I can offer you a very good and complex English for Business Course online. Please do not hesitate to contact my personal e-mail below.

Contact

Steve.bradeley@icloud.com

www.inglesozinho.com

www.ingramcontent.com/pod-product-compliance
Lightning Source LLC
Chambersburg PA
CBHW081947070426
42453CB00013BA/2276

* 9 7 8 1 4 6 8 9 5 5 7 2 9 *